Endow
Educating on the Nature & Dignity of Women

Pope John Paul II's

Letter to Women

An Introduction to the "New Feminism"

A commentary by Erica Laethem

Ascension Press
West Chester, PA

Nihil Obstat: Mr. Steve Weidenkopf
                    Censor Deputatus

Imprimatur: +Most Reverend Charles J. Chaput, O.F.M. Cap.
                    Archbishop of Denver
                    August 22, 2006

Published by Ascension Press
Post Office Box 1990
West Chester, PA 19380
Orders: 1-800-376-0520
www.AscensionPress.com

Cover design: Devin Schadt

Printed in the United States of America

ISBN: 978-1-932927-80-1

CONTENTS

Come, Holy Spirit, fill the hearts of Your faithful and enkindle in them the fire of Your love.

Send forth Your Spirit and they shall be created. And You shall renew the face of the earth.

O God, Who instructs the hearts of the faithful by the light of the Holy Spirit, grant us in the same Spirit to be truly wise, and ever to rejoice in His consolation. Through Jesus Christ, our Lord.

Amen.

chapter 1

Introduction

John Paul II

The world response to the death of Pope John Paul II on April 2, 2005 came as a surprise to some in the secular media. In a modest Vatican apartment overlooking St. Peter's Square, aglow with candlelight and the solemn fervor of the thousands who came to keep vigil, John Paul II finally went home. For the first time in history, the entire world tuned in to the coverage of the death and funeral of a pope via television, radio, and the Internet. The international interest left many reporters stumped: What was it about this man that the news of his failing health drew so many people—many of them young people—to camp outside his papal apartment on St. Peter's Square to pray and show their solidarity with a man whose ailing body rendered him immobile and mute? What was it about this man that enticed some 3.5 million pilgrims to Rome from every inhabited continent to stand in line for sixteen hours or more to pay homage to him and brought 200 heads of state together for his funeral Mass?

In an effort to understand and explain the world's extraordinary response many people of good will in the secular media put forth depictions of the greatness of John Paul II in terms with which they were familiar. Often, he was portrayed as a glorified diplomat who delivered a message of peace and tolerance "despite" his Catholicism, just as Mother Teresa of Calcutta has been relegated to a glorified social worker who served the poor "despite" her faith in Christ. Yet the greatness of John Paul II was not that he was like the world, but rather that he was very *unlike* it. As the English writer G.K. Chesterton put it,

> The Saint is a medicine because he is an antidote. Indeed that is why the saint is often a martyr; he is mistaken for a poison because he is an antidote. He will generally be found restoring the world to sanity by exaggerating whatever the world neglects, which is by no means always the same element in every age. Yet each generation seeks its saint by instinct, and he is not what the people want, but rather what the people need.[1]

Did you know?

The first Pope was St. Peter the Apostle, a Galilean fisherman-turned disciple who was commissioned by Christ to be the leader of the Apostles and the head of the Church on earth after his crucifixion. Jesus called him Peter and said "on this rock I will build my church" (Mt 16:18). He told Peter he would give him the "keys of the kingdom of heaven" and told him "whatever you bind on earth shall be bound in heaven and whatever you loose on earth shall be loosed in heaven" (Mt 16:19). After the death of Christ, St. Peter relocated to Rome, where he died a martyr's death. From that point onward, the successors of Peter have been entrusted with the role of the "Servant of the Servants of God," as Vicar of Christ on earth. The title "pope,'" used since the fourth century to refer to the successor of Peter, means "father" in its Greek linguistic roots. As the Second Vatican Council teaches, the Holy Father is the "perpetual and visible principle and foundation of unity of both the bishops and of the faithful" (*Lumen Gentium*, 23), which includes nearly one billion Catholics around the world.

NOTES

---

1 G.K. Chesterton, *St. Thomas Aquinas and St. Francis of Assisi* (San Francisco: Ignatius Press, 2002), pp. 22-23.

Immolated: Killed as a sacrificial victim

Ideology: A systematic body of concepts, especially about human life or culture

Pontificate: The office or term of a pope

Encyclical: A letter written by the Pope to his brother bishops throughout the world. They can also be addressed to priests, lay people, and all men and women of good will.

NOTES

In an age wrought by the denigration of human life, John Paul II was a champion of the human person. Born Karol Józef Wojtyla in Poland in 1920, he witnessed first-hand the devastating effects of Communist rule. He spoke out against a Marxist idealism which reduced man in his concrete form into something abstract and denied the existence of a transcendental law to which one could appeal in order to determine what is good and what is evil. Deprived of his identity and uniqueness, man became an "anonymous sacrificial victim, **immolated** upon the altar of **ideology**."[2] When man is dissolved into an abstract entity, everything is considered licit. Those in power have no scruples about sacrificing millions of human beings because the end justifies the means, even the most vicious ones.[3] And while Communism was annihilating the concrete man in the East, another type of absolutist tendency was devaluing man in the West. Unbridled liberal capitalism, which treats humans as "merchandise" whose value can be measured for what they have or the functions they can perform or how "useful" they are to the rest of society, was gaining force in the more developed, wealthier nations.

From the very beginning of his **pontificate**, John Paul II spoke and wrote extensively in defense of the intrinsic dignity of man as male and female. He believed that the greatest problems facing the modern world were rooted in an inadequate understanding of the inestimable worth of each and every human person. But his conviction that each and every human life—whether male or female, rich or poor, young or old, Christian or non-Christian, black or white—is sacred and must be protected as such was not a conviction "despite" his Christian faith; rather, it was precisely because of it. In his very first papal **encyclical**, *Redemptor Hominis* (The Redeemer of Man), he recalled the words of the Second Vatican Council:

> Christ ... in the very revelation of the mystery of the Father and of his love, *fully reveals man to himself* and brings to light his most high calling ... Human nature, by the very fact that it was assumed, not absorbed, in him, has been raised in us also to a dignity beyond compare. For by his Incarnation, he the son of God, *in a certain way united himself with each man*. He worked with human hands, he thought with a human mind. He acted with a human will, and with a human heart he loved.[4]

2 The philosophy of Karl Marx (1818-1883) was the driving force for the Communist totalitarianism that rampaged through Eastern Europe, China and parts of Latin America over the last century. Ironically, his philosophy arose "as a defense of man against the tyranny of God." See Ramon Lucas Lucas, LC, *L'Uomo, Spirito Incarnato* (Torino, Italy: Edizioni Paoline, 1993), p. 11, in English, *Man, Incarnate Spirit: A Philosophy of Man Compendium*, trans. Nikola Derpick, LC and Stephen Arndt, ed. Alex Yeung, LC and Stephen Arndt (New York: Circle Press, 2005), pp. 6-7.
3 Ibid.
4 John Paul II, Encyclical Letter on the Redeemer of Man, *Redemptor Hominis* (Boston: Daughters of St. Paul, 1979), 8, citing Vatican Council II, Pastoral Constitution on the Church in the Modern World *Gaudium et Spes* (December 7, 1965), 22

In the **mystery** of the **Incarnation**, Jesus Christ did not do away with human nature, but redeemed it and elevated it so that each person can share in "the very life of God,"[5] thus revealing the dignity of each human person. John Paul II saw the proclamation of this truth as the antidote to the world's erroneous philosophies. It was precisely because of his belief in the Christian teaching of the Incarnation that John Paul II defended the dignity of the human person.

At the heart of the mystery of the Incarnation of Christ there is a woman (cf. Gal 4:4): the Blessed Virgin Mary. Our late Holy Father had a particularly deep devotion to Our Lady. His own mother died when he was only eight years old. His devotion to our Blessed Mother was so strong that he entrusted his entire pontificate to her with the commitment, *Totus Tuus*, a Latin expression which means, "I am entirely yours." His love for the Mother of God seemed to flavor every aspect of his pontificate. Even his papal crest bore the mark of his loyalty to her, adorned with a prominent initial *M* standing at the foot of the crest's cross. Some have said that his relationship with Our Lady played a role in his special sensitivity for woman and the challenges facing all women in the modern age.

A **mystery** is "a concrete something that when you bump into it, it puts you in contact with a divine reality" (Jeremy Driscoll, OSB, *What Happens at Mass* [Chicago: Liturgy Training Publications, 2005], p. 3)

The **Incarnation** is the act in which God took on human flesh in the person of Jesus.

John Paul II's Papal Crest

NOTES

DISCUSSION QUESTIONS

1. In his twenty-six years as "Servant of the Servants of God," John Paul II touched billions of hearts. How will you remember him?

2. John Paul II championed the immeasurable worth of each and every human person. What are some modern-day worldviews that threaten that dignity?

3. What do you expect to find in this letter? Why?

---

5 John Paul II, Encyclical Letter on the Gospel of Life, *Evangelium Vitae* (Boston: Daughters of St. Paul, 1995), 2. See 2 Peter 1:4

Ontological: Relating to or based upon being or existence.

∞

Written to Me (*Read no. 1 of the Letter to Women*)

Pope John Paul II begins his *Letter to Women* with the salutation, "I greet you all most cordially, women throughout the world!" The *Letter to Women* is written to all women—not just Catholic women or Christian women or married women or single women or rich women or literate women—but to all women throughout the world.

Not only is John Paul II speaking to women as a collective, but he is speaking directly "to the heart and mind of every woman." It's as though he has hand-written a personal letter to each one of us, scrawled out our home address on the face of the envelope, sealed the flap with hot blue wax and his papal crest, and sent it off at the Vatican post office. Today, we open our mailboxes to find this sincere and reflective "thank you" letter.

In his personal note, he tells us that he is giving thanks to God and to each of us for the gift of our femininity. He wants us to know how important we are for the Church and for the world. He invites each of us to reflect with him "on the problems and the prospects of what it means to be a woman in our time," with special consideration of the essential issues of the *dignity* and *rights* of women.

What is dignity? All things have value, to a greater or lesser extent. But only *persons* have dignity. Value can be determined by the one assigning value. Think, for example, of your favorite music group. How much would you pay for a ticket to see them in concert? Would your neighbor be willing to pay as much as you would? Tickets to the same concert may be worth $500 to one person and only $10 to another. The value of the ticket is not inherent to the ticket (the ticket—and the paper and ink it is made of—is probably only worth a few pennies); the ticket's value is determined by persons and circumstances outside of itself. Dignity, on the other hand, lies within the person. It is inherent, inalienable, and inviolable. It cannot be measured in dollar signs or utility or quality of life. In this sense, dignity is an **ontological** worthiness. It comes with *being*, not with *having* or *doing*. Because it is not given by society or us, it cannot be taken away.

Human dignity is rooted in our created origin. For every single human person has been created in the image and likeness of God.[6] "Endowed with a spiritual and immortal soul, with intellect and with free will, the human person is from his very conception ordered to

6   *Catechism of the Catholic Church*, 1700. This and all references to the *Catechism* in this study guide are taken from what has come to be known colloquially as the "Green Catechism," the most recent revision of the *Catechism* at the date of our publication: *CCC*, 2nd ed., tr. United States Catholic Conference, Inc. (Città del Vaticano: Libreria Editrice Vaticana, 1997). In the text, the *Catechism* will be abbreviated as "the *Catechism*" or *CCC*.

God and destined for eternal beatitude."[7] Christ, in uniting his divine nature to human nature in the mystery of the Incarnation, "united himself in some fashion with every human being."[8] Not only does this saving event reveal to humanity the "boundless love of God who 'so loved the world that he gave his only Son' (Jn 3:16),[9] but also the *incomparable value of every human person*."[10] The dignity of human life finds its full significance in its supernatural calling.[11] Jesus spoke of the heart of his redemptive mission saying, "I came that they might have life, and have it abundantly" (Jn 10:10). The life of which he spoke, John Paul II points out, is a "new" and "eternal" life "which consists in communion with the Father, to which every person is freely called in the Son by the power of the Sanctifying Spirit."[12] This is the extraordinary calling of each and every human person: to share in the very divine life of the Trinity (cf. 2 Pet 1:4). Because the human person is called to "a fullness of life which far exceeds the dimensions of his earthly existence," the loftiness of man's "supernatural vocation reveals the *greatness* and the *inestimable value* of human life even in its temporal phase."[13]

Human rights are intimately connected to the dignity of the human person. "In fact," John Paul II emphasized, "the recognition of the dignity of every human being is the foundation and support of the concept of *universal human rights*."[14] Because human rights are rooted in the dignity of the human person, they are to be recognized, not destroyed or created anew. Thus, in order for solutions to the issues and problems raised by international policymakers to be honest and permanent, they must be based in *"the recognition of the inherent, inalienable dignity of women, and the importance of women's presence and participation in all aspects of social life."*[15] If rights are not formally recognized in democratic decision-making bodies as rooted in the intrinsic dignity of the human person, even democratic nations risk becoming a *tyranny of the strong over the weak*[16] where those in power decide the winners and the losers in the game of rights.

> The dignity of man rests above all on the fact that he is called to be in communion with God.
>
> *–Gaudium et Spes, 19*

Rights Talk

Mary Ann Glendon, professor of Law at Harvard University and leader of the Holy See's delegation to the Beijing Conference argues that in the last few decades, a new language of rights has led to the impoverishment of American political discourse. More recently, this language has crept onto the international level.

Its features include:

1. "Rights envisioned without corresponding individual or social responsibilities;

2. One's favorite rights touted as absolute with others ignored;

3. The rights-bearer imagined as radically autonomous and self-sufficient

4. The willy-nilly proliferation of new rights."[1]

7 *CCC* 1711.
8 Vatican II, *Gaudium et Spes*, 22.
9 All Scripture quotes are taken from the Revised Standard Version – Catholic Edition.
10 John Paul II, *Evangelium Vitae*, 2.
11 Ibid., 2.
12 Ibid., 1.
13 Ibid., 2.
14 John Paul II, "Welcome to Gertrude Mongella, Secretary General of the Fourth World Conference on Women (May 26, 1995)," 2, in *The Genius of Women* (Washington, D.C.: NCCB/USCC, 1997), p. 38, emphasis John Paul's.
15 *Ibid.*, emphasis John Paul's.
16 In *Evangelium Vitae*, John Paul II writes, "When a parliamentary or social majority decrees that it is legal, at least under certain conditions, to kill unborn human life, is it not really making a 'tyrannical' decision with regard to the weakest and most defenseless human beings? Everyone's conscience rightly rejects those crimes against humanity of which our century has had such sad experience. But would these crimes cease to be crimes if, instead of being committed by unscrupulous tyrants, they were legitimated by popular consensus?" (*EV*, 70.)

1 Glendon, "What Happened at Beijing," p. 35. For more on this topic, see Mary Ann Glendon, *Rights Talk: The Impoverishment of Political Discourse* (New York: Free Press, 1991).

DISCUSSION QUESTIONS

1. Today, we have opened a personal letter from Pope John Paul II to each of us. Before coming today, did you know that there was a letter waiting in your mailbox from our late Holy Father addressed personally to you? As you begin to read it, how do you feel?

2. What are some of the common measuring devices the culture in which we live uses to try to assign a value to human life?

3. What are some of the ways that basic human rights are endangered today?

4. What are some ways that we, as women, can help to promote the dignity and rights of women where we live and throughout the world?

The State of the World

John Paul II wrote *Letter to Women* on the eve of the Fourth World Conference on Women held in Beijing by the United Nations in 1995. In anticipation of this conference, Pope John Paul II declared 1995 the "Year of the Woman." On January 1, 1995, he dedicated his World Day of Peace message to the theme "Women: Teachers of Peace." Throughout the year, he devoted over fifteen Sunday **Angelus** reflections to developing his distinctive, dynamic feminism. His letter to us, the *Letter to Women* that we are studying in this course, is the centerpiece of a series of papal statements about women given that year.[17] With it, he invites us to join in an ongoing dialogue between the Church and the UN about a new manifestation of the assault on human dignity that he described as "the evil of our times."[18] As we prepare to join in this conversation, it will be helpful for us to look back and recall the events and issues leading up to and happening at the time John Paul II wrote this letter.

In the twenty years preceding the **1995 Beijing Conference** the UN hosted three other conferences on women. The first one was held in 1975 in Mexico City, the second one in 1980 in Copenhagen, and the third in 1985 in Nairobi. The purpose of the fourth conference in Beijing was to implement the call for the "removal of all obstacles to women's full and equal participation in development in all spheres of life."[19] With the theme of "Equality, Development and Peace," the Beijing Conference roused hopes of helping to bring about the genuine promotion of the status of women throughout the world. However, another UN conference held one year earlier in Cairo—the International Conference on Population and Development—promoted (unsuccessfully) abortion on demand as a means of population control, and this raised concerns that the Beijing Conference would be used by population reduction advocates with unfinished business from Cairo to revisit the abortion on demand issue. John Paul II and the **Holy See** delegation feared that for these advocates "getting rid of poverty" meant "getting rid of poor people."[20]

The **Cairo Conference** was the third in a series of international population conferences. The first was convened in 1974 in Budapest and the second was held in Mexico City in 1984. In his article "What Really Happened at Cairo," papal biographer George Weigel explains that the most powerful planners of these committees

The **Angelus** is a prayer which meditates on the Annunciation, the Blessed Virgin Mary's response to the message of the archangel Gabriel, and the Incarnation. Every Sunday afternoon, John Paul II prayed the Angelus from his apartment window with the pilgrims gathered below. In addition to the prayer, he would give a reflection on a topic he considered particularly pertinent at that time. During the Easter Season, the prayer Regina Caeli would replace the usual Angelus.

For additional information regarding the **Beijing & Cairo Conferences**, see the appendices at the end of this study guide.

The Holy See

In international relations, the Pope and the Roman Curia are known as "the Holy See." The term *See* denotes *diocese*. The diocese of Rome is also a recognized state, the State of Vatican City. It is commonly referred to as the Holy See since it is the place of the martyrdom of St. Peter, the first pope.

The Holy See has a unique role at the United Nations. While the Catholic Church does not see herself as having a direct role in partisan politics, she "wants simply *to promote a human state*. A state which recognizes the defense of the fundamental rights of the human person, especially of the weakest, as its primary duty."[1] In fidelity to Christ and promotion of human freedom, "[t]he Church *proposes; she imposes nothing.*"[2] At the UN, the Holy See has Permanent Observer status, which means that it is a non-voting member that can raise concerns and speak up when proposals threaten vulnerable populations who cannot speak up for themselves.

1 John Paul II, *Evangelium Vitae*, 101, citing his to Address to Participants in the Study Conference on "The Right to Life in Europe" (December 18, 1987): *Insegnamenti X*, 3 (1987), 1446.
2 John Paul II, Encyclical Letter on the Permanent Validity of the Church's Missionary Mandate Mission of the Redeemer *Redemptoris Missio* (1990) (Boston: Daughters of St. Paul, 1990), 39.

17 For the complete texts of John Paul II's 1995 messages to and about women, see *The Genius of Women* (Washington, D.C.: NCCB/USCC, 1997).
18 Letter from Cardinal Wojtyla to Henri de Lubac, February 1968, as cited in Lubac, *At the Service of the Church*, trans. Anne Elizabeth Englund (San Francisco: Ignatius Press, 1993), p. 172
19 "Fourth World Conference on Women Conference Brochure (16 June 1994);" available from www.un.org/Conferences/Women/PubInfo/brochure.txt; Internet; accessed 12 November 2005.
20 Mary Ann Glendon, "What Happened at Beijing," in *First Things 59* (January 1996): p. 34.

Eugenics is "the study of agencies under social control that may improve or impair the racial qualities of future generations, whether physically or mentally."[1]

The eugenics movement is devoted to "purifying the human species" through controlling factors in procreation. In this case, the controllers aimed to "improve" the human race by directing their eugenic efforts towards Latin America, Africa and Asia.

The UN Declaration of Human Rights

The Holy See's involvement at the UN often involves encouraging the UN to keep the commitment it made in December 1948 with the Universal Declaration of Human Rights. The Preamble of the Declaration recognizes "the inherent dignity and of the equal and inalienable rights of all members of the human family" as "the foundation of freedom, justice and peace in the world."

Article 3 recognizes that "Everyone has the right to life, liberty and the pursuit of happiness."

Article 16(1) states that "Men and women of full age, without any limitation due to race, nationality or religion, have the right to marry and to found a family."

Article 16(3) provides that "The family is the natural and fundamental group unit of society and is entitled to protection by society and the State."

Article 25(2) grants that "Motherhood and childhood are entitled to special care and assistance."[2]

generally held the belief that people were "essentially a problem, even a pollutant, rather than a resource; that social, political, economic and ecological catastrophe was right around the corner unless drastic steps were taken to stabilize and then reverse the world population trends."[21] Given this worldview of the global situation, population control advocates were seeking to force implementation of extensive population reduction campaigns which included abortion on demand in the name of family planning. Many of these advocates were willing to overlook the Chinese policy of coercive abortion, demonstrating the lengths to which they were willing to go to obtain their objective. But coercive government programs did not appeal to the supposed beneficiaries of "population control," namely, the countries of the developing world. Third World countries pleaded for protection, retorting that development, not population control programs imposed by wealthy nations, would improve their situation.[22]

At the Cairo Conference, the United States delegation led the crusade for abortion and **eugenic** population control programs, pushing all other population and development issues to the background. The Holy See, on the other hand, was a vocal defender of the dignity of the person and the need for programs to promote development in Third World countries. Mary Ann Glendon, professor of law at Harvard University and the leader of the Holy See's delegation for the Beijing Conference, expressed her concern that "the Holy See's efforts to correct that skewed emphasis never got through to the public. For the most part, the press accepted the population lobby's caricature of the Vatican at Cairo as anti-woman, anti-sex, and in favor of unrestrained procreation."[23] Recognizing that the Church's teachings on women were often misrepresented or poorly understood and that the Beijing Conference could help to improve the status of women in the world, John Paul II purposely declared 1995 the "Year of the Woman" and dedicated much of his teaching and writing to this theme. John Paul II also met with Mrs. Gertrude Mongella, the Tanzanian woman who was to be the Secretary General of the upcoming Beijing Conference. They spoke about the struggles of many women, the need for women's participation in all areas of public life, the exploitation of women and the need to protect life at every stage and in every situation. After the encounter, Mrs. Mongella told the press, "If everyone reasoned like he did, perhaps these kinds of meetings would no longer be necessary."[24]

1   This definition was given by the *Eugenics Review* is cited by Germaine Greer, *Sex and Destiny* (London: Secker and Warburg, 1984), p. 259.
2   General Assembly of the United Nations, *Universal Declaration of Human Rights* (December 10, 1948) (United Nations Department of Public Information, 1998), hereafter *Universal Declaration of Human Rights*.

21 George Weigel, "What Really Happened at Cairo," in *First Things* 50 (February 1995): p. 24. For a more on the Cairo Conference and John Paul II's reactions to it, see Weigel, *Witness to Hope: the Biography of Pope John Paul II* (New York: HarperCollins Publishers, Inc., 2001), pp. 715-727.
22 Weigel, "What Really Happened at Cairo," pp. 24-25.
23 Glendon, "What Happened at Beijing," p. 30.
24 Mrs. Mongella spoke to the Italian Catholic daily, *Avvenire*. See "Worldwatch," *Catholic World Report*, August/September 1995, p. 7.

DISCUSSION QUESTIONS

1. In his letter to us, John Paul II says he would like to "dialogue" with us and reflect with us on "the problems and the prospects of what it means to be a woman in our time." As a woman, what do you consider the most important concerns for women in our day? Consider yourself and women from the developing world. If you were a delegate to the United Nations, what priorities would you address?

2. The *Universal Declaration of Human Rights* recognizes "the inherent dignity" and "the equal and inalienable rights of all members of the human family" as "the foundation of freedom, justice, and peace in the world." It recognizes that "everyone has a right to life, liberty, and the pursuit of happiness" and provides that "the family is the natural and fundamental group unit of society and is entitled to protection by society and the State." It also entitles motherhood and childhood special assistance. In what ways might the efforts at the conferences which preceded the Beijing Conference have threatened fundamental human rights?

NOTES

A "Letter" to Women

The form of this document is a "letter." The Church uses various written forms to communicate her teachings (dogmatic and pastoral constitutions, decrees, encyclical letters, and apostolic letters, among others). In writing this letter to women, John Paul II is continuing the apostolic tradition of writing letters to communicate the Church's teaching and apply it to current situations.

There is a hierarchy among the various church documents and letters. The most important papal letters are encyclicals, which are addressed to the bishops of the Church and also often to the entire world. Encyclicals are papal acts in the form of letters and express the Pope's ordinary teaching authority.[25] "Its contents are presumed to belong to the ordinary magisterium unless the opposite is clearly manifested."[26] An example of an encyclical would be John Paul II's *Evangelium Vitae (The Gospel of Life)*. Apostolic letters are addressed to particular groups of people, such as a group of bishops or priests and are the second most important papal letter. These letters contain social and pastoral teachings of the Church.[27] Typically, apostolic letters have significant teaching authority, and we are taught to read these documents with the intention of full obedience. An example of an apostolic letter would be John Paul II's *Mulieris Dignitatem (On the Dignity and Vocation of Women)*.

Additionally, there are many forms of papal announcements: Holy Thursday letters to priests, letters written to different communities, various homilies, television and radio messages. *The Letter to Women* would be included among these forms of writings. All these messages are used to explain various points of the Church's teaching and are commonly used to respond to events, which take place around the world.[28] The *Letter to Women* is a great example of how the Church responds to modern issues, problems, and international events.

25 Francis G. Morrisey, O.M.I., *Papal and Curial Pronouncements: Their Canonical Significance in Light of the Code of Canon Law*. Faculty of Canon Law, Saint Paul University (Ottawa, 1995): pg. 11.
26 Ibid.
27 Ibid.
28 Ibid.

DISCUSSION QUESTIONS

1. When John Paul writes a *Letter to Women*, he is following in an apostolic tradition of writing letters to exhort and teach the Christian people. Look up the First Letter of St. Peter in Scripture and read sections of this letter from our first pope. In this letter the first pope exhorts these believers to follow Christ more faithfully, and among other things, he speaks to them about how they are to relate to the emperor and governor as well as to the other peoples (the Gentiles) around them. How would the first Christians have received Peter's letters? How will we receive our letter from John Paul II?

2. Have you ever read any other Church documents before this one? If not, what are your thoughts as you begin this first document? If you have read other Church documents, which ones? Which document(s) have been your favorites?

NOTES

chapter 2
Giving Thanks

As our Holy Father's *Letter to Women* unfolds, it begins to take the shape of one of the most worthwhile spiritual aides in the history of the Church—an examination of conscience. In an **examination of conscience**, we review our thoughts, our words, and our actions and take account of the things that would please God and those which would hurt him, ourselves, and those around us. St. Ignatius of Loyola, the founder of the Society of Jesus (the Jesuits), put forth a simple method for an examination of conscience in his "Spiritual Exercises" with the following five points: First, we thank God for all he has given us. Second, we ask for his grace to know and correct our faults. Third, we review our past, noting the faults we have committed in word, deed, thought, and by omission.[1] Fourth, we ask for God's pardon. Fifth, we propose an amendment in our lifestyle to bring about change in our life.

At the opening of his address to us, John Paul II begins by expressing his gratitude to God and to women. Throughout the next few weeks, we will see the completion of John Paul II's letter and its examination of conscience. In today's study, we will continue to read the "thank you" letter we received from him last week, with a personal statement devoted to each one of us, expressing gratitude for living out our vocation in our particular states of life. We will begin to explore our mission and vocation and look to Our Lady as a model of the Christian call to openness, generosity, and trust.

Thanks be to God *(Reread the last paragraph of no. 1)*

John Paul II begins his dialogue with us by giving thanks to God. He speaks on behalf of the entire Church, praising the Triune God for the "mystery of woman," for all that we are and all that God has accomplished in us and through us.

> #### DISCUSSION QUESTION
> Reflecting back on human history, what are some of the "great works of God" that have been accomplished in and through women?

Do try this at home!

Frequent personal **examination of conscience** is a helpful way to grow in virtue and holiness. Each day, focus on growing in one virtue or attacking one vice. At the beginning of the day, ask God for the grace to please him in all you do that day and to give you the strength to grow in that virtue or to combat that vice. Around noon, take a moment to consider your progress and renew your resolution.

At the end of the day, examine your conscience:

1. Thank God for all he has given you.
2. Ask for the grace to know and correct your faults.
3. Review the hours of the day, noting faults in word, deed, thought or omission.
4. Ask for God's pardon.
5. Propose an amendment.

St. Ignatius suggested that we impose some small penance upon ourselves for each time we break our resolution. By the end of the week, we hope that by God's grace, we will have improved our ways.

NOTES

---
1 We fail by omission when we fail to do what we should do.

Fiat: Latin for "let/may it be done."

Grace is a favor, the free and undeserved help that God gives us to respond to his call and to become children of God, adoptive sons, partakers of the divine nature and of eternal life.

–*CCC 1996*

NOTES

Cooperating with Grace *(Read Luke 1:26-38. Read the first paragraph of no. 2)*

Jesus Christ, through the gift of himself, brings about the mystery of salvation. This gift of salvation reaches back and shines its first light *in and through* a woman: God himself took on human flesh through the person of the Blessed Virgin Mary so that the world might be redeemed. We must understand that Mary in the Incarnation was not a passive recipient but *an active participant* in the saving work of God in the Incarnation of Christ. Mary, like all who share in a human nature, was endowed with an intellect and a free will. The Lord did not force his love on her, but like a young man on bended knee, he proposed to give her that which was most precious to him—a gift of himself.[2] And she freely consented with her resounding ***fiat***!

The significance of Mary's *fiat* is not to be underestimated. The future of humanity hinged upon her response. "'Behold, I am the handmaid of the Lord; let it be done to me according to your word.'[3] This was the moment of Mary's vocation. The very possibility of Christmas hung upon this moment."[4] Likewise, we are all invited to imitate Mary by surrendering our lives, our own flesh and blood, and all that we are, to allow Christ to fill us with his Presence so that he may work *in* us and *through* us. He proposes his love to us, and he lets us choose to say, "Yes! Fiat! I do!"

It is not surprising, then, that John Paul II's first word of thanks to the Almighty is intimately connected with his expression of gratitude towards women. Ultimately, it is from our Creator that all graces flow, but at the same time, it is up to us to openly receive his gifts and cooperate with his **grace**.

In his thanksgiving, John Paul II introduces the themes of the *vocation* and *mission* of women. A vocation is a calling or an invitation. It is a gift, initiated by God, and freely received by the person called. When we hear the term *vocation* in the context of the Church, we usually think of a religious vocation, such as the calling to the priesthood and religious life, yet this understanding of vocation, however true, is reductive. The word *vocation* is derived from the Latin term *vocare*, which means "to call out." A vocation is a calling, an invitation. It's a gift, initiated by God and freely received by the one to whom the invitation is extended. Each one of us has a vocation, for Christ *calls* each one of us and says, "Follow me" (Cf. John 1:12-18; Romans 8:14-17; 2 Peter 1:3-4).

---

2   With all due respect to the Almighty, lower-case pronouns are used in this study when referring to our Lord to be consistent with the quotations from the encyclicals of John Paul II.
3   Lk 1:38
4   John Paul II, "Homily for the Mass of the Students of the Pontifical Roman Minor Seminary (December 20, 1981)." Translated from the Italian version by the author. Italian version available from http://www.vatican.va/holy_father/john_paul_ii/homilies/1981/documents/hf_jp-ii_hom_19811220_seminario-minore_it.html; Internet, accessed 12 November 2005.

John Paul II also speaks of our *mission*. The term mission is derived from the Latin word *mittere*, meaning "to send off." Not only does the Lord *call* each of us into a profoundly personal and life-giving relationship with him, but he also desires to *send us off*, so that we, too, might participate in sharing his love with others. Each of us, like the Blessed Virgin Mary, has a unique and specific mission on this earth that only we can fulfill. What is yours?

DISCUSSION QUESTIONS

1. All Christians are called to imitate Mary's *fiat*! We are called to imitate her openness, her generosity and her trust. What was Mary open to?

2. How generous was she?

3. Why was she able to be so generous?

4. In whom did she place her trust?

5. Read together the *Catechism*, no. 967. As a young Jewish woman, what must Mary's relationship with God have been like for her to trust him in such a radical way?

NOTES

1   See Vatican II, *Gaudium et Spes*, 24. I owe this summary to Fr. John Riccardo, the former director of the Cardinal Maida Institute in Plymouth, Michigan. He uses a similar one in his presentation on John Paul II's Theology of the Body. These talks can be accessed via Internet at www.stanastasia.org/id25.html, accessed 12 November 2005.

A Gift of Self *(Read to the end of no. 2.)*

Most of us have never received a thank you letter quite like this one, one that thanks us for "all that we represent in the life of humanity" as mothers, wives, daughters, sisters, and consecrated women. How often do we hear the praise of women in careers to the belittlement of stay-at-home moms? Or disapproving remarks to mothers who have no choice but to work outside the home? How often do we witness an infatuation of famous or sexy women with a disinterest in the girl next door? John Paul II's unique appreciation for us is rooted in a profound understanding of the nature and vocation of woman.

An understanding of the *nature* of woman is the foundation for an understanding about the *vocation* of woman. We share in a human nature that is common to all human beings, and thus, we share in a vocation that is common to all members of the human family. As women, we share in a specifically female embodiment of human nature, and thus, are invited to a specifically feminine vocation that can be lived out in countless ways.

Sacred Scripture tells us that all those who share in human nature have been created *in the image and likeness of God (cf. Gn 1:26-28)*. If there is a likeness between our nature and God's nature, and if an understanding of our nature helps us understand our vocation, it would be worthwhile for us to understand what divine nature is like. This begs the question, "What is God like?" Such an inquiry has been the topic of philosophical and theological discussion since the beginning of time. Thankfully, we have not been left in the dark to grapple with this question on our own. God has revealed himself in the person of Jesus Christ. Jesus tells his disciples, "He who has seen me has seen the Father" (Jn 14:9).

One thing that God has revealed about himself is that he is a Trinity— one God in three persons. In this union of persons, the Father, out of his infinite goodness, generosity, and love, gives everything he is to the Son. The Son, in turn, returns everything he is to the Father, holding nothing back for himself. This intense exchange of love between the Father and the Son is the Holy Spirit.

When Jesus prayed to the Father, "that they may all be one ... even as we are one" (Jn 17:21-22), he implied a certain likeness between the union of the divine Persons, namely the Father, the Son, and the Holy Spirit, and the relationship between God's sons and daughters on earth. This likeness between us and the Trinity reveals that "man ... cannot fully find himself except in a sincere gift of himself."[5]

5   Vatican Council II, *Gaudium et Spes*, 24.

By making of ourselves a sincere gift to another, we come to resemble the inner life of the Trinity. We imitate, that is, a life of perpetual self-giving. We have been created out of love by God who calls us to love in return. "To love," states the *Catechism*, "is the fundamental and innate vocation of every human being."[6] Christians are called to self-giving love through a life of beatitude, for we are all called to holiness.[7] And holiness, we must remember, is not just for priests and nuns; it is a call for each one of us, whether we are married, single or consecrated, working or staying at home. The Second Vatican Council's *Dogmatic Constitution on the Church (Lumen Gentium)* underscored this point with great emphasis. In fact, the Council dedicated an entire chapter to the theme "The Universal Call to Holiness in the Church." In it, we are reminded that "all the faithful of Christ, of whatever rank or status, are called to the fullness of the Christian life and to the perfection of charity" so as to promote a "more human manner of living" through holiness. To reach this "perfection," we must "use [our] strength accordingly as [we] have received it, as a gift from Christ." We must "follow in his footsteps and conform [ourselves] to his image, seeking the will of the Father in all things" and "devote [ourselves] with all [our] being to the glory of God and the service of [our] neighbor."[8] This is the vocation of every Christian.

As women, the Lord invites us to live out our Christian vocation to self-giving love in a variety of ways that are common to our female embodiment of human nature.[9] Our specifically female vocation is not so much concerned with the jobs that we can do or the tasks that we can perform; rather, it is concerned more with how we exist as women. Dr. Pia de Solenni[10] described this core message of the New Feminism as, "Whatever she does, she does as a woman, not a genderless creature." In his bouquet of praises, the Holy Father acknowledges the many contributions of women who have made of themselves gifts to others.

As our Holy Father thanks each of us for all that we represent in the life of humanity, we should let his gratitude be a starting point for our own examination of conscience. Let us thank God for the gift of our femininity, ask him to help us know and correct the ways we have not used it to love, then ask for God's forgiveness for those times, and make a resolution for how we can bring our feminine gifts to enrich our families and society at-large.

Man...cannot fully find himself except in a sincere gift of himself.
—*Gaudium et Spes, 24*

NOTES

6   *CCC* 1604.
7   See *CCC* 2013.
8   *Lumen Gentium*, 40.
9   For more on the particular dimensions of the fulfillment of the female personality, see John Paul II, *Mulieris Dignitatem*, 17.
10 In 2001, John Paul II granted Dr. Pia de Solenni the Pontifical Prize for the Academies "for her work in Thomistic theology," citing her doctoral dissertation, *A Hermeneutic of Aquinas's Mens Through A Sexually Differentiated Epistemology: Towards An Understanding Of Woman As Imago Dei*. She is now the director of life and women's issues at the Family Research Council in Washington, D.C.

NOTES

DISCUSSION QUESTIONS

In the first chapter of his *Confessions*, St. Augustine writes, "Thou hast made us for Thyself, O Lord, and our hearts are restless until they find their rest in thee."[11]

1. What are some of the ways we try to satisfy our hunger for love?

2. Do these things fulfill us? Why or why not?

3. Where in our lives can we imitate Mary's *fiat* to let God, who is Love, fill us with his love?

4. Where and in what ways can we make of ourselves sincere gifts to others? Think of some concrete examples.

11 A modern translation reads "[Y]ou have made us for yourself and our hearts find no peace until they rest in you." St. Augustine, *Confessions*, tr. R.S. Pine-Coffin (London: Penguin Books, 1961), p. 21.

To Mothers

In his July 16, 1995 Sunday Angelus address, John Paul II celebrated the Vocation to Motherhood, emphasizing the desperate need of society to restore a profound appreciation for women who choose to be mothers:

> The fact can never be sufficiently stressed that woman must be appreciated in every area of her life. However, it must be recognized that, among the gifts and tasks proper to her, her vocation to motherhood stands out particularly clearly. With this gift woman assumes almost a 'foundational' role with regard to society. It is a role she shares with her husband but it is indisputable that nature has assigned to her the greater part. I wrote about this in *Mulieris Dignitatem*: 'Parenthood—even though it belongs to both—is realized much more fully in the woman, especially in the prenatal period. It is the woman who 'pays' directly for their shared generation, which literally absorbs the energies of her body and soul. It is therefore necessary that the man be fully aware that in their shared parenthood he owes a special debt to the woman' (no. 18).
>
> Woman's singular relationship with human life derives from her vocation to motherhood. Opening herself to motherhood, she feels the life in her womb unfolding and growing. This indescribable experience is a privilege of mothers, but all women have in some way an intuition of it, predisposed as they are to this miraculous gift.
>
> The maternal mission is also the basis of a particular responsibility. The mother is appointed guardian of life. It is her task to accept it with care, encouraging the human being's first dialogue with the world, which is carried out precisely in the symbiosis with the mother's body. It is here that the history of every human being begins. Each one of us, retracing this history, cannot fail to reach that moment when he began to exist within his mother's body, with an exclusive and unmistakable plan of life. We were 'in' our mother, but without being confused with her: in need of her body and her love, but fully autonomous in our personal identity.

The woman is called to offer the best of herself to the baby growing within her. It is precisely by making herself a "gift," that she comes to know herself better and is fulfilled in her femininity. One could say that the fragility of her creature demands the best of her emotional and spiritual resources. It is a real exchange of gifts! The success of this exchange is of inestimable value for the child's serene growth.

...In [Mary], the vocation to motherhood reached the summit of its dignity and potential. May the Blessed Virgin help women to be ever more aware of their mission and encourage the whole of society to express every possible form of gratitude and active closeness to mothers![12]

DISCUSSION QUESTIONS

1. How is the vocation to motherhood viewed in our society? Why?

2. How does a mother make of herself a "gift" to her children?

---

12 John Paul II, "The Vocation to Motherhood" (July 16, 1995), 1-3, in *The Genius of Women*, pp. 25-27.

To Every Woman

Celibacy: Virginity as a state of life.

∞

NOTES

The Holy Father gives thanks to wives, who live out their vocation to love in marriage. The Catholic vision of marriage is one of mutual self-giving. Husbands are commanded to lay down their lives for their wives as Christ laid down his life for the Church in a self-sacrificial love. Wives, in turn, are invited to let their husbands love them and to make of themselves a gift to their husbands in return. A vision of marriage in which the husband dominates the wife as a CEO does a company or a master his slave, or in which the wife's role is reduced to servitude and obedience is **not** an authentically Catholic vision of marriage; rather, a Catholic marriage calls both husband and wife to "be subject to one another out of reverence for Christ" (Eph 5:21).[13]

In his Apostolic Exhortation on *The Role of the Christian Family in the Modern World (Familiaris Consortio)*, John Paul II writes, "The future of the world and the Church passes through the family."[14] The family becomes an *ecclesia domestica* (a domestic church) where faith meets action and we learn to live in virtue and self-giving love. In the loving relationship between mothers and daughters, fathers and daughters, sisters and sisters, and brothers and sisters, the feminine presence in the family enriches all its members and ultimately, all of society.

John Paul II underscores the desperate need for an authentically feminine presence in every aspect of life and society. One of the characteristics of our female embodiment of human nature is an intense desire to integrate our minds and our hearts. When we know something, we do not simply want to know it in our heads, but we want to know it with everything that we are. We have a tremendous capacity for empathy. When someone is hurting, we hurt with them. When someone is experiencing joy, we rejoice with them. We see persons beyond structures and policies or ideologies. We do not want to separate knowledge from reality or concrete experience. We are endowed with a special capacity and responsibility to transform society into one which is more humane.

Our Holy Father gives thanks to those women who have consecrated themselves to the Lord at the service of his Church. They live virginity as a state of life in imitation of Christ, who taught the value of celibacy and lived it himself. Christian **celibacy** is not imposed but chosen freely in response to a special grace and calling from God. Not everyone is called to live virginity as a state of life, but

13 John Paul II, in his Apostolic Letter On the Dignity of and Vocation of Women, emphasizes "All the reasons in favor of the 'subjection' of woman to man must be understood in the sense of a 'mutual subjection' of both 'out of reverence for Christ.'" John Paul II, Apostolic Letter On the Dignity of and Vocation of Women, *Mulieris Dignitatem* (Boston: Daughters of St. Paul, 1988), 24.
14 John Paul II, Apostolic Exhortation on The Role of the Christian Family in the Modern World, *Familiaris Consortio* (Boston: Daughters of St. Paul, 1981), 75.

some are chosen to do so for the sake of the kingdom of heaven.[15] Women who choose virginity confirm the riches of their femininity by making a sincere gift of their whole lives to Christ, the Spouse of their souls.

As his masterpiece of gratitude accelerates to the finale, John Paul II lands on this glorious major chord: Thank you, *every woman*, for the simple fact of being a *woman*! By bringing the gifts of femininity to every area of life and society, we help to humanize our culture and build a civilization of love.

Discussion Question

The gift of our femininity is something innate in our nature but also something that we can stifle or develop. How can we help to nourish this gift in ourselves, in our moms, sisters, daughters, and girlfriends?

Questions for Personal Reflection

1. Do I value every vocation as a gift from God, or do I treat some as more important than others in the way I think, speak, or act?

2. Do I appreciate the other women in my life?

3. How do I show my appreciation for them? Could I do more to encourage them?

For Personal Meditation

Man...cannot fully find himself except in a sincere gift of himself.

—Gaudium et Spes, *24*

---

15 Cf. Matthew 19:3-12.

chapter 3

Obstacles, Consequences, and Solutions

A few weeks ago, we lifted the papal seal on an envelope to find a letter written by John Paul II to each one of us. In it, the Holy Father told us that he was giving thanks to the Most Holy Trinity on behalf of the entire Church for the "mystery of woman" and for each one of us. Then, acknowledging that all graces from the Lord require our cooperation in order to bear fruit, he recognized the many ways women have chosen to make themselves "sincere gifts" to others. He thanked us for enriching the world's understanding of human relations with the gift of our femininity. In doing so, his letter to us began to take the form of an examination of conscience, a spiritual aide whose five points always begin with a genuine offering of praise and gratitude.

As the *Letter* continues, John Paul II identifies obstacles, consequences, and solutions to women's full development. He starts with an introspective examination, accepting objective blame when it is due to the members of the Church, expressing regret and sorrow for all its members, and renewing a commitment to turn to Christ to set women free from exploitation and domination. Only after he looks inwardly at the Church and its members does he address other obstacles that have historically stood in the way of women's full development, obstacles which desperately need to be removed in order to build a society of justice and a civilization of love.

NOTES

Lust, as the Holy Father uses the term, means using another person for one's own pleasure.

NOTES

Beg Your Pardon *(Read the first paragraph of no. 3)*

In a marriage between a man and a woman, the words "thank you" are of great importance. But few relationships would skim the surface of human depth if conversations only consisted of giving thanks. Our own human experience tells us that when we enter into relationship with another, whether it is romantic or friendship, we are bound to encounter situations and decisions that demand more dialogue. In the course of human relationships, we falter, we stumble, we hurt one another, and we say, "I'm sorry." We ask forgiveness, and we think and talk about ways we can prevent the same thing from happening again. Likewise, the marriage relationship between Christ and his Bride, the Church, would be stuck at a superficial level if in her dialogue with her Lord and Bridegroom she simply stopped at "thank you" and never examined past shortcomings with a contrite spirit that desires to set things right.

"Unfortunately," writes the Holy Father, "we are heirs to a history which has *conditioned* us to a remarkable extent. In every time and every place, this conditioning has been an obstacle to the progress of women." This is one of the themes John Paul II took up at the beginning of his pontificate in his 129-homily series on the "theology of the body." In it, he traces the roots of the "battle of the sexes" to the very beginning, to the relationship between Adam and Eve as depicted in Genesis.

The original relationship between the first couple was one of mutual trust and self-giving; it was free from shame—even in nakedness—and free from **lust**. In the original relationship, neither partner objectified or reduced the other to a mere instrument for pleasure; rather, both found fulfillment in making of themselves sincere gifts to the other and always sought the good of the other. But with the Fall, in which the first couple freely chose to reject the Lord's loving plan, the relationship between man and woman was forever marred by sin. For the first time, Adam and Eve felt shame of their bodies, and they hid from God. The once clear understanding that they were to be a gift to each other became muddled and the human heart became "a battlefield between love and lust."[1] For man, shame united to lust became an impulse to "dominate" the woman.[2] He began to consider the woman as an object to gain possession of and not as a gift, and in doing so, he condemned himself to becoming only an object for her, and not a gift.[3] "If this impulse prevails on the part of the man," writes John Paul II, "the instincts that the woman directs

1   John Paul II, General Audience of July 23, 1980. English translation from *The Theology of the Body: Human Love in the Divine Plan* (Boston: Daughters of St. Paul, 1997), p. 125.
2   As confirmed in the phrase, "He shall rule over you" (Genesis 3:16). Ibid., General Audience of June 25, 1980, p. 123.
3   Ibid., General Audience of July 30, 1980, p. 128.

to him can have a similar character. Sometimes, they precede the man's 'desire,' or even aim at arousing it and giving it impetus."[4] For both the first man and the first woman, self-giving was replaced by selfishness. A spirit of love was replaced by a spirit of competition.

4   John Paul II, *Theology of the Body*, p. 123.

Concupiscence: Human appetites or desires which remain disordered due to the temporal consequences of original sin, which remain even after Baptism, and which produce an inclination to sin.[1]

Confession: A Sacrament of Healing "The Lord Jesus Christ, physician of our souls and bodies, who forgave the sins of the paralytic and restored him to bodily health, has willed that his Church continue, in the power of the Holy Spirit, his work of healing and salvation, even among her own members."[2] The purpose of the sacrament of Penance, or "going to confession" is healing. When we receive the sacrament, it is God who forgives our sins.[3] At the same time, "Christ has willed that in her prayer and life and action his whole Church should be the sign and instrument of forgiveness and reconciliation that he acquired for us at the price of his blood."[4] Since Christ entrusted to his apostles the ministry of reconciliation, it is their successors (bishops and priests, the bishop's collaborators), that have the power to forgive sins "in the name of the Father, of the Son, and of the Holy Spirit."[5]

NOTES

The First Fall *(Read together the Catechism, 397-398)*

As heirs to the first couple, we have inherited the disorder of **concupiscence**; that is, we have a weakness, a sickness, a tendency to fall. We desire the good and we want to do what is right, yet at the same time, we have trouble attaining it because we are easily distracted by the pursuit of things that claim to be good and fulfilling but leave us feeling quite the opposite. And the same "I" that knows and desires the good, chooses to throw itself into self-destruction.[5] The relationship between man and woman has been disordered by concupiscence, so that in "every time and place," as John Paul II writes, this conditioning has been "an obstacle to the progress of women."

The consequences have been devastating, both to women themselves and to humanity as a whole. As concupiscent injustices are institutionalized in political and social systems, women have often been treated as second-class citizens or even slaves. Not only has this prevented women from being themselves, it has also resulted in what our Holy Father calls "a spiritual impoverishment of humanity." Note the gravity of the consequence John Paul II identifies. For it is only when we are truly free to live in accordance with the dignity that is ours by virtue of our humanity that we can make of ourselves sincere gifts to the world.

"If objective blame," the Holy Father writes to us, "has belonged to not just a few members of the Church, for this I am truly sorry." As a penitent before a priest in **confession**, the Holy Father kneels in the place of those members of the Church, asking forgiveness from God and from us. Every Sunday, in the Creed at Mass, we profess that the Church, which is the Mystical Body of Christ, is one, holy, catholic, and apostolic. We can say this because the Church was born anew by the blood and water that flowed from the side of Christ at his death and continues to be sanctified through the blood that he shares with us in the Eucharist under the appearance of wine. At the same time, the Church is comprised of sinful people who have made mistakes and are in need of forgiveness.

For forgiveness and freedom from the corruption of sin, John Paul II turns to the *attitude of Jesus Christ himself*. For a model of how we ought to live, he turns to the One who loves us so much that he gave his very life for us. "When it comes to setting women free from every kind of exploitation and domination, the Gospel contains

1   Glossary of the *CCC*, "Concupiscence," p. 871
2   *CCC* 1421
3   Because only God has the power to forgive sins. See the *CCC* 1441. Cf. Mark 2:7.
4   *CCC* 1442.
5   *CCC* 1461.

5   Joseph Pieper clarifies, "Most difficult to grasp is the fact that it is indeed the essential human self that is capable of throwing itself into disorder to the point of self-destruction. For man is not really a battlefield of conflicting forces and impulses which conquer one another; and if we say that the sensuality 'in us' gets the better of our reason, this is only a vague and metaphorical manner of speaking. Rather it is always our single self that is chaste or unchaste, temperate or intemperate, self-preserving or self-destructive. It is always the decisive center of the whole, indivisible person by which the inner order is upheld or upset. 'It is not the good my will preserves, but the evil my will disapproves, that I find myself doing' (Rom. 7, 19).' Josef Pieper, *The Four Cardinal Virtues* (Notre Dame: University of Notre Dame Press, 1966), pp. 148-149.

an ever relevant message which goes back to the *attitude of Jesus Christ himself.*" In the gospels, we see that Christ's openness, respect, acceptance, and tenderness towards women were overtly counter-cultural.

Take, for example, Jesus' encounter with the Samaritan woman at the well (cf. Jn 4:7-27). Samaritans and Jews were hardly friendly neighbors. The Jews despised the Samaritans. They were considered to be idolaters, and Jews were forbidden even to touch a utensil used by a Samaritan. Jesus, in breaking all religious and gender codes, speaks with her, asks for water from *her* ladle, reveals himself to her, and invites her to become his disciple.

We can also look at Christ's interaction with the woman who hemorrhaged for twelve years (Mk 5:35-34). In Jewish tradition, the loss of blood was identified with uncleanness. Women who were menstruating, for example, were considered ritually unclean and they were bound by rules regarding interactions with others. Jesus, in his merciful love, not only cures her, but takes her by the hand!

We can also see that women were given pride of place in the Incarnation, the Passion and the Resurrection of Christ. Christ's interactions with women will be studied in greater detail in ENDOW's *Mulieris Dignitatem* study, in which John Paul II describes the Lord's attitude as one which was a "consistent protest against whatever offends the dignity of women."[6] He treated women with the dignity and honor they have as daughters of God.

6   John Paul II, *Mulieris Dignitatem*, 5.

NOTES

1. We are heirs to a history which has marred the relationship between man and woman and at times has stood as an obstacle to women's full development. What are some of the ways we still see the consequences of concupiscence today in the "battle of the sexes"?

2. For each of the scenarios discussed in Question 1, Christ is the solution. Discuss how and in what ways each of the relationships you identified would look different if it were to be restored in Christ to a relationship of mutual self-giving love and trust.

3. John Paul II asks, "How much of [Jesus'] message has been heard and acted upon?" What do you think?

Examining the Past *(Read the 2nd paragraph of no. 3 and the 1st paragraph of no. 4)*

Upon completion of his introspective examination of conscience and request for forgiveness, John Paul II looks outwardly to review the history of humanity. "Women have contributed to that history as much as men and, more often than not, they did so in much more difficult conditions," he observes. The need to incorporate women's contribution to history is a theme that he frequently took up in his 1995 statements on women. He states "it would be appropriate to rewrite history in a less one-sided way. Unfortunately, a certain way of writing history has paid greater attention to extraordinary and sensational events than to the daily rhythm of life, and the resulting history is almost only concerned with the achievements of men. This tendency should be reversed."[7] He proceeded to speak on behalf of the Church "to pay homage to the manifold, immense, although frequently silent, contribution of women in every area of human life."[8]

John Paul II was an avid and vocal proponent of equal opportunities for men and women in every area, including education. In his letter to us, you can almost hear the sorrow in his voice as he remembers those women who had a love for culture, art, and science, but who were frequently "at a disadvantage from the start, excluded from equal educational opportunities, underestimated, ignored, and not given credit for their intellectual contributions." Throughout his pontificate, he recognized great and saintly women in history whose influence shaped the lives of successive generations.

One such woman was Maria Montessori, for whom the famous "Montessori" schools are named. In 1970, upon the centennial of her birth, Pope Paul VI remarked "that the secret of her success, in a certain sense the very origin of her scientific merits, should be sought in her soul or in that spiritual sensitivity and feminine outlook which enabled her to make the 'vital discovery' of the child and led her to conceive of an original form of education on this basis (cf. *Insegnamenti di Paolo VI*, VIII [1970], 88)."

John Paul II continued, "The name Montessori is dearly representative of all women who have made important contributions to cultural progress. Unfortunately, in looking objectively at historical reality, we are compelled to notice with regret that even at this level, women have suffered the effects of systematic marginalization. For too long opportunities for expression outside the family have been denied or restricted, and the women who,

7   John Paul II, "History Needs to Include Women's Contributions (July 30, 1995)," 1, in *The Genius of Women*, pp. 28-29.
8   Ibid.

despite being thus penalized, succeeded in asserting themselves have had to be very enterprising."[9] It was time, he said, to close the gap between the cultural opportunities for men and women.

The Holy Father lived the message he preached. Among those women working at the Vatican is Natalia Tsarkova, a Russian-born painter who was commissioned to be John Paul II's official portrait painter. In an interview with *Inside the Vatican*, she told the reporter that she was the only woman in her painting class at Moscow's Fine Arts Academy. The director of the Academy told her that "he'd believed that women belonged in the kitchen and the nursery and not to the painting studio." All that changed when the director met Natalia, whose talent forced him to rethink his opinion about women artists.[10] When John Paul II writes that he thinks "particularly of those women who loved culture and art," perhaps he had his own portraitist in mind.

John Paul II was not estranged to the common person. As a young pastor, he would go kayaking with couples and young people and listen to them share the joys and the struggles of their daily lives and relationships. As he grew older and became cardinal and pope, he maintained close relationships with friends and was in constant dialogue with lay men and women throughout the world. All of this kept his awareness of the challenges facing women.

Among the obstacles to women's full integration into social, political, and economic life is the ever-growing prevalence of discrimination against women who have chosen to be wives and mothers. Despite the fact that humanity owes its very survival to these women, John Paul notes "the gift of motherhood is often penalized rather than rewarded."

His concern was well-warranted. When he wrote the *Letter To Women* in 1995, organizations like the UN were growing increasingly out-of-touch with the concerns facing most women. The disconnected character of the 1994 Conference on Population and Development in Cairo sent a signal to the world that the satellite of international policymaking was beginning to spin out of the orbit of reality. One would think that a conference whose theme was so closely related to marriage and whose decisions would affect primarily women would at least allude to marriage. But this was not the case. The only time the word appeared was in the chapter on "the family," in a passage condemning "coercion and discrimination in policies and practices related to marriage."[11]

9   John Paul II, "Closing the Gap between Cultural Opportunities for Men and Women (August 6, 1995)," 1, in *The Genius to Women*, p. 31.
10 Lucy Gordan, "Natalia Tsarkova 'There is light inside of the Holy Father,'" *Inside the Vatican* magazine, April 2005.
11 Weigel, "What Really Happened at Cairo," p. 27.

In her review of the 1995 Beijing Conference, Mary Ann Glendon reported that by reading the conference preparation drafts, "one would have no idea that most women marry, have children, and are urgently concerned with how to mesh family life with participation in broader social and economic spheres."[12] She likened the overall effect to the "leaning tower of Pisa, admirable from some angles, but unbalanced, and resting on a shaky foundation."[13] At the conference, a minority coalition led by the European Union (which also included Barbados, Canada, Namibia, and South Africa), "contested every effort to include the word 'motherhood' except where it appeared in a negative light."[14]

The predominant advocate groups at the "Beijing + 5" and "Beijing + 10" Conferences, held in 2000 and 2005 respectively, continued to push a paradigm that negates, rather than protects motherhood. This is a significant diversion from the UN's own Universal Declaration of Human Rights, which provides that "Motherhood and childhood are entitled to special care and assistance."[15]

In a world of justice and equality, motherhood and citizenship would not be considered mutually exclusive or even mildly opposed. Neither would being a woman imply a refusal of personal rights. On the contrary, writes John Paul II, "there is an urgent need to achieve *real equality* in every area: equal pay for equal work, protection for working mothers, fairness in career advancements, equality of spouses with regard to family rights, and the recognition that everything that is part of the rights and duties of citizens in a democratic state."

In addition to promoting an equal opportunity for men and women to work outside the family, he also advocates the necessity of society to "respect the right and duty of a woman as mother to carry out her specific tasks in the family, without being forced by need to take an additional job." [16] Women should not be made to feel guilty for wanting to work in the home and nurture and care for their children, but rather they should be "recognized, applauded, and supported in every possible way."[17] John Paul II goes as far as to say that humanity is so indebted to those women who have chosen to be mothers that the state has a "duty" to facilitate financial provision for financial security for women who choose to stay home with their children.[18]

12 Glendon, "What Happened at Beijing," p. 30.
13 Ibid.
14 Ibid., p. 32.
15 *Declaration of Human Rights*, Article 25(2).
16 John Paul II "Equal Opportunity in the World of Work" (August 20, 1995) 2, in *The Genius of Women* p. 32-33.
17 John Paul II, "Welcome to Gertrude Mongella," 3, in *The Genius of Women*, p. 39.
18 John Paul writes, "[T]he state has a duty of subsidiarity, to be exercised through suitable legislative and social security initiatives." See John Paul II, "Welcome to Gertrude Mongella," 8, in *The Genius of Women*, p. 42. According to Fr. Thomas Williams, LC, STD, Dean of Theology at the Pontifical University Regina Apostolorum in Rome, "duty of subsidiarity" in this context can be properly understood as facilitating financial provision. Fr. Thomas Williams, interview with Erica Laethem, November 9, 2005, in Rome.

NOTES

1. How do these words from John Paul II's *Letter To Women* speak to you?

   "Yet how many women have been and continue to be valued more for their physical appearance than for their skill, their professionalism, their intellectual abilities, their deep sensitivity; in a word, the very dignity of their being!" (*Letter To Women*, 3)

2. For those of us who are mothers and caregivers, what do you like most about your work?

Justice and Necessity *(Read the second paragraph of no. 4)*

Often, we hear proponents of the equality between men and women promote their platforms on the principles of social justice. John Paul II goes even further, saying that real equality in every area is not only a matter of justice, but also a matter of *necessity*. The world *needs* women and the gift of our femininity in every area of life. His argument does not follow the usual path of "sameness," which tends to promote some variation on the idea that we're all the same, and therefore, it shouldn't matter if the job is done by a man or a woman. Rather, he affirms that society needs women *precisely because* women are different from men and bring complementary and much needed gifts.

In a Sunday Angelus reflection dedicated to the topic of "The Feminine Genius," John Paul II spoke of the necessity to recognize the role of women, not only in the family circle, but also in the wider context of all social activities:

> Without the contribution of women, society is less alive, culture impoverished, and peace less stable. Situations where women are prevented from developing their full potential and from offering the wealth of their gifts should therefore be considered profoundly unjust, not only to women themselves but to society as a whole ... [I]t is necessary to strive convincingly to ensure that the widest possible space is open to women in all areas of culture, economics, politics, and ecclesial life itself, so that all human society is increasingly enriched by the gifts proper to masculinity and femininity.[19]

By our very nature as women, we have a gift for humanizing every place we find ourselves. Our involvement in many spheres of life will expose the contradictions of a society organized solely according to the criteria of efficiency and productivity. John Paul II points to a number of areas where our feminine insight will provide solutions to problems looming in the immanent future, including leisure time, the quality of life, migration, social services, euthanasia, drugs, health care, and ecology. By sharing, rather than snuffing, the gifts that are naturally ours, we can help redirect society's prerogatives and institutional priorities to transform our culture into one which is more humane. In doing so, we play a vital role in building a "civilization of love."

---

19 John Paul II, "The Feminine Genius (July 23, 1995)," 1, in *The Genius of Women*, p. 27.

NOTES

1. How does John Paul II's emphasis of the necessity of women's involvement differ from the usual secular social justice arguments?

2. Where in our culture today can we identify the results of "a society organized solely according to the criteria of efficiency and productivity"?

3. What are some practical ways that we can help to make these areas ever more worthy of humanity?

The Heinous Act of Sexual Exploitation
(Read all of no. 5)

With strong conviction, John Paul II presents an intense appeal to "vigorously condemn" sexual exploitation and violence against women as well as the "widespread hedonistic and commercial culture" which encourages the systematic exploitation of sexuality and corrupts even young girls into letting their bodies be used for profit.

We seem to live in a culture that is juxtaposed between two extremes: At one extreme is the exaggeration that "our bodies are everything." This view promotes an unhealthy obsession with weight, figure, and sex appeal, and tends to neglect the spiritual dimension of the person. At the other extreme is the misunderstanding that "our bodies have nothing to do with who we are," that they are arbitrary material that has nothing to do with our identity. Therefore, as the logic goes, what we do with our bodies, or what happens to our bodies, does not affect us. It's just physical matter. We can abuse them and use them in any way we want because they are detached from who we are. In philosophy, this extreme is called *dualism*, which was made famous by Descartes' famous phrase, "I think, therefore I am." It's the idea that the intellect is somehow disassociated from the body and that people are simply "thinking things."

The dualism of Cartesian philosophy has been consistently rebuked by both Catholic and secular thinkers since it was first proposed. Dr. William May of the John Paul II Center for Marriage and Family in Washington, D.C. explains:

> When God created man, he did not create a "conscious subject" to whom he then, as an afterthought, gave a body. Rather, in creating man, "male and female he created them" (Gen 1:27)—that is, as bodily, sexual beings. Moreover, when God the Son became man, he became flesh (*sarx egeneto*; Jn 1:14)...According to this integral vision of the human person, a living human body is a person, and every living human body, born or preborn, consciously aware of itself or crippled by severe mental handicaps so that it is not capable of consciousness, is a *person*, a being of surpassing goodness.[20]

Between these two extremes is another understanding of the human person, supported by science, philosophy, and the Catholic faith. In

---

20 William E. May, *Marriage: The Rock on Which the Family is Built* (San Francisco: Ignatius Press, 1995), pp. 81-82.

this view, the human person is an integral union of body and soul; it is impossible to divorce the two or to treat people as material bodies without souls or as disembodied intellects. As a result, for example, the crimes of sexual exploitation and rape cannot be condemned with enough disgust, for they touch the very core of the victim, not only her body.

John Paul II punctuates the point that before blame for these despicable crimes is placed on women, these acts are indeed "crimes" for which guilt needs to be attributed to men and to the complicity of the general social environment. Upon hearing the news of such crimes in our own culture, how often do we hear people excuse the attacker, "Well, she shouldn't have been out that late ..." or "She was asking for it..." or "If she'd hadn't been wearing that outfit ..." or "She should have known better than to be hanging around with that crowd ..." or "She shouldn't have been walking alone..." while ignoring the fact that her offender made a choice to act as he did? In such situations, a woman is too often blamed and then left alone. We must also recognize those heroic women who have given birth to a child conceived in rape. These women deserve great respect.

John Paul II brings our attention to those women who are suffering today—not only in foreign, war-stricken areas, but also in prosperous and peaceful societies which permit practices that "aggravate tendencies towards aggressive male behavior." At the 2005 follow-up "Beijing + 10" Conference on the Status of Women held in New York , the topics of sex trafficking and prostitution roiled the second half of the conference. Countries in which prostitution is legal and whose economies depend upon sex tourism and the sex trade stood staunchly against attempts to slow their business. They were supported by some of the old-line, hard-line feminist groups who pushed individual autonomy at all costs, neglecting how prostitution affects women, families, and societies. Other traditional feminist groups joined those promoting the "New Feminism" and a brigade of other nations standing on the side of poor women and the developing world— the most convenient victims for the commercial sex trade.

Prostitution is inherently harmful and dehumanizing, and it fuels human trafficking, a form of modern-day slavery. Statistics show that of the estimated 600,000 to 800,000 people trafficked across international borders, 80 percent of the victims are female and 50 percent are children.[21] Eighty-nine percent of women in prostitution want to escape.[22] Sixty to seventy-five percent of women in prostitution have been raped and 70-95 percent have been physically assaulted.[23] Where prostitution has been legalized or tolerated, there is an increase in demand for sex slaves.[24] Yet countries like the Netherlands (Holland) and Germany continue to support a sex industry whose victims are generally the poor, the young, minorities, those with a history of abuse, and those with little family support.[25]

In preparation for Beijing in1995, the Holy Father called upon the conference to underscore the magnificence of human sexuality and give it the special protection it deserves:

> The trivialization of sexuality, especially in the media, and the acceptance in some societies of a sexuality without moral restraint and without accountability, are **deleterious** above all to women, increasing the challenges that they face in sustaining their personal dignity and their service to life. In a society which follows this path, the temptation to use abortion as a so-called 'solution' to the unwanted results of sexual promiscuity and irresponsibility is very strong. And here again it is the woman who bears the heaviest burden: often left alone, or pressured into terminating the life of her child before it is born, she must then bear the burden of her conscience which forever reminds her that she has taken the life of her child (cf. *Mulieris Dignitatem*, no. 14).[26]

John Paul II called for a "radical solidarity" with women, which would require "that the underlying causes which make the child unwanted be addressed. There will never be justice, including equality, development, and peace, for women or for men, unless there is an unfailing determination to respect, protect, love and serve life—every human life, at every stage and in every situation (cf. *Evangelium Vitae*, nos. 5, 87)."[27]

When looking at these problems, we cannot help but feel the pain of those women who have suffered the devastating effects of rape, abortion, and other forms of sexual exploitation and violence. We have friends, neighbors, colleagues, family members, and fellow parishioners who have been touched by these experiences. For some of us, the discussion is even more personal.

Deleterious: Harmful often in a subtle or unexpected way.

NOTES

21 U.S. Department of State, Bureau of Public Affairs, "The Link Between Prostitution and Sex Trafficking" (Publication distributed at the Beijing + 10 Conference on the Status of Women in New York, March 2005).
22 Melissa Farley et al. 2003 "Prostitution and Trafficking in Nine Countries: An Update on Violence and Post-traumatic Stress Disorder," Journal of Trauma Practice Vol. 2, No. 3/4: 33-74; and Melissa Farley, Prostitution, Trafficking, and Traumatic Stress (New York: Harworth Press, 2003).
23 Ibid.
24 Victor Malarek, *The Natashas: Inside the New Global Sex Trade* (New York: Arcade Publishing, 2004).
25 Dorchen A. Leidholt, "Demand and Debate," (Amherst, Massachusetts: Coalition Against Trafficking in Women, 2005), p. 9.
26 John Paul II, "Welcome to Gertrude Mongella," 7, in *The Genius of Women*, p. 42-43.
27 Ibid., p. 43.

NOTES

In his encyclical *Evangelium Vitae (On the Gospel of Life)*, 99, our Holy Father writes:

> I would now like to say a special word to *women who have had an abortion*. The Church is aware of the many factors which may have influenced your decision, and she does not doubt that in many cases it was a painful and even shattering decision. The wound in your heart may not yet have healed. Certainly what happened was and remains terribly wrong. But do not give in to discouragement and do not lose hope. Try rather to understand what happened and face it honestly. If you have not already done so, give yourselves over with humility and trust to repentance. The Father of mercies is ready to give you his forgiveness and his peace in the Sacrament of Reconciliation. You will come to understand that nothing is definitively lost and you will also be able to ask forgiveness from your child, who is now living in the Lord. With the friendly and expert help and advice of other people, and as a result of your own painful experience, you can be among the most eloquent defenders of everyone's right to life. Through your commitment to life, whether by accepting the birth of other children or by welcoming and caring for those most in need of someone to be close to them, you will become promoters of a new way of looking at life.

DISCUSSION QUESTION

How can we answer the Holy Father's call to show "radical solidarity" with women who have suffered these experiences?

For Personal Reflection

Have you allowed the Father of mercies to give you his forgiveness and peace?

chapter 4

Evaluating the Progress of Women's Liberation

John Paul II began his letter by giving thanks to God for women and by thanking us for cooperating with God's grace to enrich the world with the gift of our femininity as mothers, wives, daughters, and sisters, as working and consecrated women. Then, he identified obstacles to women's full development in the history of humanity. He traced the historical "battle of the sexes" to our first parents in the Garden of Eden. When the first couple rejected God's loving plan for them, their life of mutual trust and self-giving love was replaced by one of shame, fear, and self-asserting lust. "Using" became the seductive enemy of "loving." Thereafter, human beings would be tempted by the allure of making "the other" an object to be used. Women, John Paul II noted, have "suffered more deeply" from the Fall and its consequences.[1] Throughout history, women have suffered domination and exploitation. The Holy Father begged our pardon and the forgiveness of the Almighty for any objective blame due to members of the Church. He called upon the world to vigorously condemn all types of violence and exploitation and to turn to Christ and his loving acceptance and understanding of women as a model for the whole Christian community. He recognized the removal of obstacles to women's full development, not only as a matter of justice but also as a matter of necessity. Women, who have an innate capacity for human relationships, will be able to expose contradictions in societies obsessed with efficiency and productivity and will be able to make civilizations ever more worthy of humanity. We play an indispensable role in what John Paul II calls the transformation of a "culture of death" into a "culture of life."

In today's study, the Holy Father expresses his admiration for those women who have affirmed the dignity of woman throughout the ages, even when they were condemned. He invites us to evaluate with him the progress of the women's liberation movement, which he himself calls a "substantially positive" journey, despite "its share of mistakes." We will look at the progress of the first three waves of the women's liberation movement in the United States over the past 150 years and discuss its strengths and weaknesses. Then, in the final step of the Holy Father's "examination of conscience," he invites us to promote a "New Feminism," which has as its focus a positive campaign for the dignity of women.

NOTES

---

1 John Paul II, "World Day of Peace Message (January 1, 1995)," 4, *in The Genius of Women*, p. 12.

The Journey of Women's Liberation *(Read the first two paragraphs of no. 6)*

On the eve of the 1995 UN Conference on the Status of Women in Beijing, John Paul II appealed to states and international institutions to "make every effort to ensure that women regain full respect for their dignity and role." In doing so, he expresses his admiration to those women of good will who have defended the dignity of womanhood by fighting for their basic social, economic, and political rights. The Holy Father recognizes the difficulties these women encountered and the courage with which they acted. There is no doubt that many of them met great opposition from men and even from other women who accused their initiative of being "extremely inappropriate, the sign of a lack of femininity, a manifestation of exhibitionism, and even a sin!"[2]

In affirming those who committed themselves to the recognition of the dignity of womanhood, the Holy Father makes it clear that activity is not the enemy of femininity. Women are not called to be passive bystanders in the course of human events, but active participants in God's plan for humanity, which includes the recognition of the inestimable worth of women in the family, in every area of society and in the Church. Yet being proactive for the cause of women will often take courage. And courage often demands that we follow our Lord beyond what is comfortable and convenient and follow him into the areas we would not dare to go on our own, trusting in his promise that he will not abandon us.

While feminist philosophies had emerged in various forms during the Renaissance and Enlightenment periods, the women's liberation movement picked up speed in the mid-1800's. Sr. Prudence Allen, RSM, Ph.D., the former chair of the department of philosophy and current philosophy professor at St. John Vianney Theological Seminary in Denver, has performed extensive research on the development of feminism in history. A detailed outline of these feminist philosophies, based on her work, can be found in the appendix at the end of this study guide.

In the United States, there have been three major waves of the women's liberation movement over the past 150 years. Each wave identified specific obstacles to women's full development. The first wave occurred in the mid-1800's. The primary objectives of this wave of feminism included property rights for women, many of whom, at the time, were not allowed to own property themselves. Women did not have the right to vote and educational opportunities were scanty, so these early feminists worked actively for suffrage rights and for women's admittance to higher levels of education. The second wave of feminism occurred in the 1920's and 1930's, when married women were denied opportunities to work outside the home. This wave focused on improving educational and employment opportunities for women.

The third wave of feminism in the United States occurred in the 1960's and 1970's and had two different orientations: radical revolution and moderate reformation. While it promoted many of the same laudable objectives as the previous waves, it had as its emphasis liberation or freedom from the feminine body. In this sense, it was a "sexual liberation." Third-wave "moderate feminism" generally promoted a unisex theory, which affirmed the equal dignity of men and women but argued there was no significant difference between the sexes, except for some inconvenient biological differences.

Third-wave "radical feminism" had as its distinguishing premise that women's bodies are the source of inequality and injustice. It promoted the thought that a woman's body, specifically her ability to bear children, stands in the way of her full development as a woman. Therefore, the argument goes, women need to free themselves from their biology in order be fully liberated. This often entailed rendering the feminine body infertile, either temporarily or permanently, so as to make it more like that of a man. It promoted chemical methods to masculinize women's monthly hormonal curves, so that the melodic feminine cadence of natural fertility and infertility was interrupted and flattened to be more like the static lines of men. This current of feminism attacked marriage and motherhood with slogans like "A woman needs a man like a fish needs a bicycle." Women became "Womyn" to remove any reference to "men." It also took up a new language of rights which imagined the rights-bearer as radically autonomous and self-sufficient and touted one's favorite rights as absolute while others were ignored. Slogans like "It's *my* body!" arguing for a "right" to abortion imagined the individual woman as entirely autonomous and neglected any rights due to the new human being growing within.

The consequences of third-wave feminism can be seen on the international political scene today. Third-wave feminist groups, led by activist non-governmental organizations like the International Planned Parenthood Federation and Planned Parenthood Federation of America, along with wealthier capitalistic nations, are imposing aggressive population control programs on other countries and have launched corresponding campaigns against marriage and motherhood. The last thirty years have also seen a strong push to remove any special protection for mothers and children at the United Nations.[3] As we endeavor towards a new wave of feminism, these initiatives are being called into question and reevaluated in light of a positive campaign for the dignity of woman.

DISCUSSION QUESTIONS

1. Who are the women in your life that you admire the most? Why?

2. As you were growing up, what did your mothers, aunts, and grand-mothers teach you—either in word or in deed—about what it is to be a woman?

3. What are some ways that states and international institutions can ensure that women gain full respect for their dignity and role?

4. In your opinion, what are some of the best characteristics about the women's liberation movement in the United States?

5. What are some characteristics of the women's liberation movement that you would like to see transformed in the next wave of feminism?

---

3 See, for example, Mary Ann Glendon, "What Happened at Beijing," and Weigel, "What Really Happened at Cairo."

Towards a New Feminism
(Read the third paragraph of no. 6)

Despite the shortcomings of the women's liberation movement, John Paul II does not propose abolishing the feminist movement. Rather, he recognizes the overall effort as a "substantially positive one" and calls upon women to promote a "New Feminism," which summons the world to "acknowledge and affirm the true genius of women in every aspect of the life of society, and overcome all discrimination, violence, and exploitation."[4] This new feminist movement "rejects the temptation of imitating models of 'male domination'"[5] which, we must not forget, is not in God's plan for the role of men but a flat-out rejection of it; rather, the "New Feminism" is one which affirms the special dignity of women.

This dignity is not only recognizable to believers, but to all human beings. It "comes from the use of reason itself," which is proper to all men and women, not only men and women of faith. St. Paul tells us in the second chapter of his letter to the Romans that we are able to understand the God's law because it is written on the heart of every human being.[6] The word of God, the Sacred Scriptures, enable us to grasp the **anthropological** basis of this truth.

The creation accounts in the first two chapters of Genesis reveal that there are two "incarnations" of being human—male and female.[7] Both are made in the image and likeness of God. The two are equal in dignity but different from one another. In the next chapter, we will delve into a deeper discussion of these complementary differences.

Because of the Fall, we have all inherited the inclination to sin and the proclivity to reduce another person to an object, and the difference between men and women has often come to be seen as a threat. We have also seen throughout history how men have dominated women and how women have, at times, acted in a way to allow themselves to be dominated. Given this historical trend, one can understand why there has been an attempt to eradicate the differences between men and women. But this has often led to a further offense against women. In an attempt to deny these differences, women are measured according to a male norm, as though the male is the "gold standard" and woman is an imperfect man. When this happens, there is a disregard for the greatness and distinctiveness that belongs to women. The New Feminism calls for the universal recognition of the dignity of women, an "effective and intelligent campaign for the promotion of women," not a denial or negation of the differences.

Anthropology is "a systematically ordered doctrine of the knowledge of man."[1]

Difference must never be grounds for discrimination of some persons within rights and freedoms that are proper to all members of the human family. The Church denounces the "intolerable custom [that] still exists of discriminating, from the earliest years, between boys and girls. If, from the beginning, girls are looked down upon or regarded as inferior, their sense of dignity will be gravely impaired and their healthy development inevitably compromised. Discrimination in childhood will have life-long effects and will prevent women from fully taking part in the life of society."[2]

NOTES

1 Immanuel Kant, *Anthropologie in pragmatischer Hinsicht*, in Kant's *Gesammelte Schriften*, vol. 7 (Berlin: Georg Reimer, 1817). In English, *Anthropology from a Pragmatic Point of View*, tr. Victor Lyle Dowdell, revised and ed. by Hans H. Rudnick (Carbondale: Southern Illinois University Press, 1978).
2 John Paul II, "World Day of Peace Message" (January 1, 1995) 8, in *The Genius of Women*, pg. 15.

4 John Paul II, *Evangelium Vitae*, 99.
5 Ibid.
6 See Romans 2:15. See also the *CCC* 1776-1777.
7 John Paul II, *Theology of the Body*, p. 48.

In his letter to Gertrude Mongella, the Holy Father writes,

> As most women themselves point out, equality of dignity does not mean 'sameness with men.' This would only impoverish women and all of society, by deforming or losing the unique richness and inherent value of femininity. In the Church's outlook, women and men have been called by the Creator to live in profound communion with one another, with reciprocal knowledge and giving of self, acting together for the common good with the complementary characteristics of that which is feminine and masculine.[8] At the same time we must not forget that at the personal level one's dignity is experienced not as a result of the affirmation of rights on the juridical and international planes, but as the natural consequence of the concrete material, emotional, and spiritual care received *in the heart of one's family.* No response to women's issues can ignore women's role in the family or take lightly the fact that every new life is *totally entrusted* to the protection and care of the woman carrying it in her womb (cf. encyclical letter *Evangelium Vitae*, 58). In order to respect this natural order of things, it is necessary to counter the misconception that the role of motherhood is oppressive to women, and that a commitment to her family, particularly to her own children, prevents a woman from reaching personal fulfillment, and women as a whole from having an influence in society. It is a disservice not only to children, but also to women and society itself, when a woman is made to feel guilty for wanting to remain in the home and nurture and care for her children. A mother's presence in the family, so critical to the stability and growth of that basic unit of society, should instead be recognized, applauded and supported in every possible way. By the same token society needs to *call husbands and fathers to their family responsibilities*, and ought to strive for a situation in which they will not be forced by economic circumstances to move away from the home in search of work.[9]

As we have seen, several feminist philosophies have treated marriage and motherhood as a barrier to women's full development. As the Sacred Scriptures illuminate for us, marriage, according to God's design, is created to be a relationship of mutual self-giving and trust. It is the effects of sin in marriage which turns the relationship into one of self-assertion and using, and which too often results in domination of women. The solution, then, is not to denounce marriage and motherhood, as so many feminists do, but rather, to turn to Christ

8 John Paul II, "Welcome to Gertrude Mongella," 3, in *The Genius of Women*, p. 39.
9 Ibid., pp. 39-40.

and let his grace penetrate and transform our marriages to become the sign and channel of love and grace they are meant to be.

We, who have been *totally entrusted* with the gift of life as women, have been given a special assignment. Making his own the words of the concluding message of the Second Vatican Council and building on them in his own writing, John Paul II addresses us with this urgent appeal:

> 'Reconcile people with life.'[10] You are called to bear witness to the meaning of genuine love, of that gift of self and of that acceptance of others which are present in a special way in the relationship of husband and wife, but which ought to be at the heart of every relationship. The experience of motherhood makes you acutely aware of the other person and, at the same time, confers on you a particular task: 'Motherhood involves a special communion with the mystery of life, as it develops in the woman's womb … This unique contact with the new human being developing within her gives rise to an attitude towards human beings—not only towards her own child, but every human being—which profoundly marks the woman's personality.'[11] A mother welcomes and carries in herself another human being, enabling it to grow inside her, giving it room, respecting it in its otherness. Women first learn and then teach others that human relations are authentic if they are open to accepting the other person: a person who is recognized and loved because of the dignity which comes from being a person and not from other considerations, such as usefulness, strength, intelligence, beauty, or health. This is the fundamental contribution which the Church and humanity expect from women. And it is the indispensable prerequisite for an authentic cultural change.[12]

In response to the third-wave egalitarian feminism which promotes the idea that women are the same as men, the New Feminism affirms that women are equal in dignity to men and must be recognized as such, but that we are not the same. Ironically, the third-wave "feminist" movement propelled the masculinization of civilization. This has led to what John Paul II called the "culture of death," in which there is more emphasis on having and doing than on being and relationship. It reduces persons to mere objects and has its roots in an inordinate preoccupation with efficiency. What is needed in response to this is a "prophetic voice"[13] to call humanity back to the

10 Closing Messages of the Council (December 8, 1965): *To Women*.
11 John Paul II, *Mulieris Dignitatem*, 18.
12 John Paul II, *Evangelium Vitae*, 99.
13 John Paul II, *Mulieris Dignitatem*, 29.

absolute priority of love which never reduces a person to an object. This is what women of the New Feminism are called to offer the Church and the world.[14] What we need is to become more human. Woman has the gifted propensity to understand and live this truth by virtue of the lived experience of her body, which is not simply an inconvenient cage she needs to free herself from, but rather, an extraordinary gift from God.[15]

The New Feminism seeks to overcome a second and related obstacle prevalent in our culture today. We, generally speaking, tend to see the body as separate to the person, as a prison of the soul. It becomes a machine or an instrument that we can manipulate for pleasure. We need only look at the degradation of women and children in pornography for a sobering example. But the human body is not separate from the person. There is no duality between body and soul, between spirit and matter. The body is not secondary or additional. Rather, the human person is an integral union of body and soul. In this intimate union, "the body expresses the person."[16] Our female bodies, then, express something about what it means to be a woman. One of the most remarkable characteristics of our bodies is the ability to make room for another person. Literally! This is not to say that our biology is our destiny, but rather that in the union of body and soul, a woman possesses particular qualities that are common to all women and different from distinctly masculine traits. Our wondrous capacity to make room for another—whether or not we have ever born, or ever will bear, children in our wombs—profoundly marks our personality. This makes women better equipped than men to call the world back to the priority of love which has the good of persons as its goal.[17]

"This journey must go on!" John Paul II writes to us. "Women have the right to insist that their dignity be respected. At the same time, they have the duty to work for the promotion of the dignity of all persons, men as well as women."[18] Jesus taught that to whom much has been given, much will be required (cf. Lk 12:48). Because we have an incredible ability to call the world back to a priority of love and of the person, John Paul II appeals to us, for the sake of all of humanity, to 'Reconcile people with life.' "It's hard to imagine a more global vocation than this one," writes Boston College philosophy professor Laura Garcia, "and it calls for the presence of women in virtually every aspect of society, public and private. Without asking women to ignore their own family and professional obligations, the Holy

14 See John Paul II, *Mulieris Dignitatem*, 30
15 I owe this summary of the Holy Father's distinctive feminism to Fr. John Riccardo's January 2002 talk "Why an All-Male Priesthood?" The audio version is available at www.stanastasia.org/id25.html; Internet; accessed 13 November 2005, hereafter Riccardo, "Why an All-Male Priesthood?"
16 See John Paul II, *Theology of the Body*, p. 40-41.
17 Riccardo, "Why an All-Male Priesthood?"
18 John Paul II, "World Day of Peace Message" (January 1, 1995), 11.

Father is urging that women mobilize in every way they can to resist the poisonous culture of death that surrounds us these days; to battle for the dignity and worth of each human being."[19]

DISCUSSION QUESTIONS

1. Had you heard of the New Feminism before today?

2. In what ways is this new wave of the women's liberation similar to the previous waves? In what ways is it different?

3. Why do earlier waves of the feminist movement hurt women when they equate "equality with men" to "sameness to men"?

4. What are some the consequences of acting as though women are "the same as men" that you have witnessed in your life?

---

19 Laura Garcia, "The Role of Woman in Society (October 2000)," available from www.iiof.es/iffd/conferencias/iffdlaurin.htm Internet, accessed 29 July 2005.

5. In addition to the condemnation of discrimination and injustices, the New Feminism calls for "an effective and intelligent campaign for the promotion of women, concentrating on all areas of women's life and beginning with a universal recognition of the dignity of women." What does this entail?

6. For the sake of the entire human family, the Church appeals with an extraordinary calling: "Reconcile people with life." What does this mean? How can we do this?

For Personal Meditation

"Reconcile people with life." You are called to bear witness to the meaning of genuine love, of that gift of self and of that acceptance of others … which ought to be at the heart of every relationship.

–John Paul II, *Evangelium Vitae, 99*

chapter 5

Ontological Complementarity

Few passages in Scripture stimulate as much eye-rolling and tension as those that have to do with the relationships between men and women. These are the passages we often hear at weddings, where references to woman's role as "helper" or "helpmate" often provoke anxiety on the part of the bride and the rest of the women in the congregation. Many modern women and men question the validity of these texts in the 21st century. Some feel these readings must be the residue of a horribly oppressive patriarchal culture in which women were treated more like children or property than persons. Or perhaps it is a last desperate attempt of the Church "to keep women in their place," so as to prevent them from being too influential in the world. To many, they sound terribly out-of-touch, out-of-date and downright insulting towards women. How could it possibly be that the Church, which claims to defend the dignity of women, continues to proclaim these readings at marriage celebrations and in her liturgy?

Few of us (although perhaps more now than in previous years) regularly read the *Catechism*, Church documents, or Scripture commentaries to help us understand the word of God. Often, we don't know where to look or what we're looking for. Perhaps we had no idea that these resources even existed. For many of us, we never knew that we have had letters from the Holy Father waiting in our mailboxes until we began this study. Or maybe we knew they were there but decided not to open them because we are afraid of what they might say. In the meantime, we have tended to take the media's word for granted about what the Church teaches about sex, women, and marriage. It must be said that most of the time those in the news media are also not well informed about what the Church actually teaches. All too often, reports are based on what they think the Church will say rather than what is actually taught.

As a result, we begin to approach the word of God with fear and suspicion. When this happens, we look elsewhere for insights about relationships. We turn to *Glamour*, *Cosmopolitan*, soap operas, the most recent Hollywood movies, or the latest self-help guru or pop psychologist. We find something that resembles what our hearts are longing for, but in a disfigured way, like the image reflected by the wavy mirrors in the "Fun House" at the amusement park. We recognize a certain similarity to ourselves, yet when we move as our skewed reflection appears to be able to, we find ourselves in an awkward jumble of limbs. So it is when we try to imitate the caricatures of relationships we often see on the printed page or the cinema screen. Ultimately, we have an innate sense that we were made for something more, something better. And we are.

When it comes to understanding the truth about woman and her mission and "role" in the world, John Paul II consistently turns to the beginning, to the creation narratives in the book of Genesis. He invites us to "reflect anew on the magnificent passage in Scripture which describes the creation of the human race and which has so much to say about [our] dignity and mission in the world." As we do so, let's ask the Holy Spirit—the One who inspired these words to be written—to inspire us to understand them.

There are two creation accounts in the first book of the Bible. Both "poetic and symbolic," the two accounts are complementary and contain profound truths. In today's short study, our endeavor to enter into the first two chapters of Genesis will be far from an exhaustive excavation of the theological riches hidden inside. Nevertheless, we will brush off a few of the gems under the cover of the first book of the Old Testament.

In his article *Male and Female He Created Them: A Summary of the Teaching of Genesis, Chapter One*, Fr. Francis Martin, Scripture scholar at the John Paul II Institute for Marriage and Family, presents the following translation of the first creation account, drawing on the descriptive language of the original Hebrew text. The Jewish people, our older brothers and sisters in the faith, had multiple names for the One God. *Elohim* (used in the first creation account) is one of the three common names for God, whereas *Yhwh* (used in the second creation account), is the proper name for God.

Back to the Beginning *(Read Genesis 1:26-28 below; and the first two paragraphs of no. 7)*

> And Elohim said: "Let us make ádám in our image, as our
> likeness, that they may rule over the fish of the sea, and the birds
> of the heavens, and the tame beasts, and all the creeping things
> on the earth." And Elohim created the ádám in his image: in
> the image of Elohim he created him/it, male and female he
> created them. And Elohim blessed them, and Elohim said to
> them: Be fruitful, be many, and fill the earth and subjugate it,
> and rule over the fish of the sea, and the birds of the heavens,
> and all the living things creeping on the earth. [1]

In this first creation account, two things are made clear: First, man
(*'ādām*) is created in the image of God; man (*'ādām*) is the only creature
created in the likeness of the Divine. Second, man *'ādām* exists as male
and female. The human person was not created androgynous. In other
words, there are two ways of being human: male and female. Both
are created in the image of God. Thus, both are equal in dignity and
worthy of utmost respect and reverence.

Fr. Francis Martin points out that what is crucial for an accurate
understanding of this text is the word "image." The Hebrew word
selem ("image") occurs in five passages of the Old Testament to describe
Adam and his relationship to God.[2] The basic idea behind the word
selem is not so much that the image bears a physical resemblance to the
thing it represents, but that the image makes present the authority of
what—or who—is imaged. In other words, *'ādām* is to be "God's vice-
regent, the embodiment of his authority here on earth."[3]

What does it mean to embody and exercise God's own authority?
Does this mean we have liberty at all-costs, with little regard for
those who stand in the way of our objectives? Fr. John Riccardo,
STL, former director of the Cardinal Maida Institute in Plymouth,
Michigan, explains, "Not infrequently, authority is understood as
the power to arbitrarily impose one's will upon another (or others). It
is commonly equated with domination and a curtailment of another's
freedom."[4] But authority, in the true sense of the word, is precisely
the opposite of that. The word itself is derived from the Latin *auctor*
(cause, sponsor, promoter, surety), from *augere* (to increase…to
enrich).[5] The nature of authority, then, "must be distinguished from

1   As translated by Fr. Francis Martin, "Male and Female He Created Them: A Summary of the Teaching of Genesis Chapter One," *Communio* 20 (1993): 244.
2   Fr. Francis Martin, "The New Feminism: Biblical Foundations and Some Lines of Development," in *Women in Christ: Toward a New Feminism*, ed. Michelle M. Schumacher (Grand Rapids, MI: Wm. B. Eerdmans, 2004), p. 142.
3   Ibid., p. 144.
4   Fr. John Riccardo, Sacred Theology Licentiate thesis "The Theological, Philosophical and Anthropological Foundations of John Paul II's Understanding of the Mutual Subordination of Husband and Wife," written under the direction of Fr. Francis Martin, submitted and approved by the John Paul II Institute for Marriage and Family in Washington, D.C. in 1999, p. 81.
5   "Authority," in *Encyclopedia of Theology: A Concise Sacramentum Mundi*, ed. Karl Rahner (London: Burns & Oates, 1975), p. 61.

power and coercion."[6] As it has been said, power "does not promote freedom, and coercion ends it."[7] True authority, on the other hand, is "always in the service of others and their freedom. Its object is always to help men to attain their full manhood."[8] It helps the other(s) to reach fulfillment.[9] It is this kind of authority that we are called to exercise as persons created in the *selem* of God.

DISCUSSION QUESTIONS

1. When Elohim (God) says, "Let us make *'ādām* in our image, as our likeness" to whom does this plurality refer?

2. Do men reveal the image of God more than women? Do women reveal the image of God more than men? Explain.

3. How can you be the *selem* of God, making present God's enriching authority?

---

6   Ibid., p. 62.
7   Ibid., p. 64.
8   Ibid., p. 62.
9   Ibid., p. 61. "There is no true authority without love, for God puts authority into the hands of men that they might be at the service of others."
     John Haas, "The Christian Heart of Fatherhood: The Place of Marriage, Authority, and Service in the Recovery of Fatherhood," *Touchstone*
     14 (2001): 47-52. As cited in Riccardo, "Mutual Subordination of Husband and Wife," pp. 81-82. See also Francis Martin, *The Feminist
     Question: Feminist Theology in the Light of Christian Tradition* (Grand Rapids, MI: Wm. B. Eerdmans, 1994), pp. 184-189, for a discussion
     of how one of the most damaging effects of the Enlightenment has been the equating of causality with domination.

Help! *(Read the last two paragraphs of no. 7)*

In the first creation account, the equality between man and woman is clear, as both are *ádám*. Having been created in the image —the *selem*—of God, both are called to make present God's own enriching authority on earth. In the second account of creation in the book of Genesis, the equality between man and woman is less obvious. In its reference to woman as "helper," this text has caused more than a few egalitarian-minded people of good will to shudder. Trusting in the Holy Spirit and the coherency of revealed truth, let us turn again to the word of God so that we may better understand what is being said.

Read the second creation narrative in Genesis 2:18-25[10] below:

> Then Yhwh God said: It is not good, the man's being alone, let me make for him a helper matching him. Then Yhwh God fashioned out of the soil all the beasts of the field, and all the birds of the heavens, and He brought them to the man to see what he would call them, and whatever the man called any living creature, that was its name. The man gave names to all the tame animals, to all the birds of the heavens, and all the beasts of the field, but for the man there was found no helper matching him.[11] The Yhwh God made a deep sleep come upon the man and he slumbered, and He took one of his ribs and closed up its place with flesh. Yhwh God built up the rib that He had taken from the man into a woman and He led her to the man. Then the man said: This at last is bone from my bone and flesh from my flesh. This one shall be called woman for from man was this one taken. For this reason a man leaves his father and mother and cleaves to his wife and they become one flesh. They were both naked, the man and his wife, but they felt no shame with one another.

Commenting upon the second creation account, John Paul II writes, *"The second description of the creation of man ...* makes use of different language to express the truth about the creation of man, and especially of woman. In a sense, the language is less precise, and, one might say, more descriptive and metaphorical. Nevertheless, we find no essential contradiction between the two texts. The text of Genesis 2:18-25 helps us to understand better what we find in the concise passage of Genesis 1:27-28. At the same time, if it is read together with the latter, *it helps us to understand even more profoundly*

10 As translated by Francis Martin in a manuscript on the biblical theology of marriage and family in the Old Testament. Cited in Riccardo, "Mutual Subordination of Husband and Wife," p. 49.
11 The idea expressed in the Hebrew by the word *kenegdô* ("matching him") is that this "helper" must be of the same kind that the man is. See Manfred Hauke, *Women in the Priesthood? A Systematic Analysis in the Light of the Order of Creation and Redemption*, tr. David Kipp (San Francisco: Ignatius Press, 1988), p. 201.

the fundamental *truth* which it contains *concerning man* created as man and woman in the image and likeness of God."[12]

"What exactly is it about this passage that can help us 'understand even more profoundly the fundamental truth' about man, male and female, as being in the image of God?" asks Fr. John Riccardo. The answer to this question seems to come in accurately understanding a word that is frequently misunderstood by saints and critics alike: "helper."[13] The English term "helper" is the translation of the Hebrew word *'ezer*. This noun is found nineteen times in the Old Testament—fifteen of those occurrences refer to *divine* aid.[14] That woman is "helper" (*'ezer*) to man, then, is not at all pejorative or degrading if this description is also used at other times to describe God himself.

"It is important to recall that up until Genesis 2:18 there has been a constant refrain uttered by God upon looking at his creation: "It is good." In fact, this refrain has been uttered seven times before Genesis 2:18. But then, for the first time, God changes his tone and says: 'It is not good.'"[15] *What* is not good? It is not good that man is alone. In order for his creation to be "good" something further must occur. John Paul II explains, "In the second account of creation, through the symbolism of the creation of woman from man's rib, Scripture stresses that humanity is not complete until woman is created."[16] In Genesis 2:18-25, God is revealing that humanity is not "complete" until the arrival of a "helper." This notion of woman as "helper" is far from belittling. John Paul II makes clear, it "should not be interpreted as meaning that the woman is man's servant – 'helper' is not the equivalent of 'servant'; the psalmist says to God: 'You are my help' (Ps 70:5; cf. Ps 115:9, 10, 11; Ps 118:7; Ps 146:5); rather the whole statement means that woman is able to collaborate with man because she complements him perfectly. Woman is another kind of 'ego' in their common humanity, which consists of male and female in perfectly equal dignity."[17]

In his letter to us, John Paul II is clear that the "help" that woman gives to man is "not one-sided, but *mutual*. Woman complements man, just as man complements woman...Womanhood expresses the 'human' as much as manhood does, but in a different and complementary way." In a July 9, 1995 Sunday Angelus Reflection, the late Pope explained, "Precisely because woman is different

12 John Paul II, *Mulieris Dignitatem*, 6.
13 Riccardo, "Mutual Subordination of Husband and Wife," p. 50.
14 See Manfred Hauke, *Women in the Priesthood?*, pp. 201, 203; Jean-Louis Ska, "'Je vais lui faire un allié qui soit son homologue' (Gen 2,18). A propos du terme 'ezer-aide,'" *Biblica* 65 (1984): 233-238; Marie de Merode, "'Une aide qui lui corresponde.' L'exégèse de Gen 2,18-24 dans les éscrits de l'Ancien Testament, du judaïsme et du Nouveau Testament," *Revue Théologique de Louvain* 8 (1977): 329-352.
15 Riccardo, "Mutual Subordination of Husband and Wife," pp. 50-51.
16 John Paul II, General Audience, Nov. 24, 1999, as reported in the English language edition of *L'Osservatore Romano*, N. 48, 1 December, 1999, hereafter General Audience, Nov. 24, 1999.
17 John Paul II, General Audience, Nov. 24, 1999.

than man, nevertheless putting herself at the same level, she can really be his 'helper.' On the other hand, the help is anything but unilateral: the woman is 'a helper' for the man, just as the man is a 'helper' for the woman!"[18]

This complementarity is not only physical and psychological, but also ontological; that is, it has to do with the order of *being*, and not just the order of *having* or *doing*.[19] In other words, the help that the woman gives the man and the man gives the woman is more than help for procreation or for managing the earth (on the level of doing). It is much more than that. The creation narratives reveal that man, for some reason, is in need of an "other," or more accurately, another "I." What Genesis 2:18-25 reveals is that humans are created for relationship. As Fr. Francis Martin succinctly says, "He needs 'help' to be human."[20]

This is one of the ways in which we are created in the image of God. In addition to being in the likeness of God as rational, free, and self-possessed, we are also relational, just as God, in his simplest form, is a pure relationship between the members of the Trinity, each of whom is equal in worth and distinct from the others. The relationship between the Father, the Son and the Holy Spirit is one of pure self-giving love. God the Father, desiring to share all of his goodness, pours himself out completely to God the Son. The Son receives the Father's love and returns it by giving himself completely back to the Father in love. This eternal, mutual outpouring of love between the Father and the Son is the Holy Spirit. John Paul II refers to the Spirit as "the Person-Love."[21] "Such love is characterized by its motivation: it is wishing well to a beloved for the beloved's, not the lover's sake."[22] It is not self-seeking, but seeks the good of the other. It is precisely this kind of love and communion that we are called to mirror. This is the solution to the distorted reflection of love that we find in pop magazines and Hollywood movies. This is what we were created for: to share in the very divine life of God,[23] a life of perpetual self-giving. We get there by loving God and by loving one another, by "helping" one another to reach fulfillment.

18   John Paul II, "Complementarity and Reciprocity between Men and Women (July 9, 1995)," 2, in *The Genius of Women*, p. 24.
19   See Sr. Prudence Allen, RSM, PhD, "Philosophy of Relation in John Paul II's New Feminism," in *Women in Christ* 67-104, esp. p. 94.
20   Francis Martin, unpublished manuscript on the biblical theology of marriage and family in the Old Testament. In Riccardo, "Mutual Subordination of Husband and Wife," p. 52.
21   John Paul II, *Dominum et vivificantem*, 10.
22   Mary Rousseau, "Pope John Paul II's Letter on the Dignity and Vocation of Women: The Call to Communio," *Communio* 16 (1989): 215. See also, Karol Wojtyla, "The Family as a Community of Persons," in *Person and Community: Selected Essays*, trans. Theresa Sandok, OSM (New York: Peter Lang, 1993), p. 317.
23   See 2 Peter 1:4

NOTES

1. What is the significance of woman being made out of the same "stuff" as man?

2. What is the significance of woman being created out of man's rib, and not his head or his foot?

3. How does the marital relationship between a man and a woman reflect the relationship between the Divine Persons of the Trinity?

4. How does a priest or a consecrated person mirror the interior life of Trinity?

1 + 1 > > 3 *(Read no. 8)*

Humanity is fully realized only through the complementarity of man and woman, who have shared equality and shared responsibility, both in procreation and in stewardship of the earth. Speaking of the complementarity of man and woman, the Holy Father adds, "The most intense expression of this reciprocity is found in the spousal encounter in which the man and the woman live in a relationship which is strongly marked by biological complementarity, but which at the same time goes far beyond biology. Sexuality in fact reaches to the deep structures of the human being, and the nuptial encounter, far from being reduced to the satisfaction of a blind instinct, becomes a language through which the deep union of the two persons, male and female, is expressed. They give themselves to one another in this intimacy, precisely to express the total and definitive communion of their persons, they make themselves at the same time the responsible coworkers of God in the gift of life." [24]

One of the most exciting philosophical developments in recent years has been on this very topic of the *integral gender complementarity* between men and women. In the history of philosophy and feminism there have been three basic models used to explain the relationship between man and woman: gender unity, gender polarity, and gender complementarity. (For further study, see the outline and reference chart in the appendix at the end of this study). *Gender unity,* which has Plato as one of its first postulators, claims that there is no significant difference between men and women. The body is held to be unimportant and man and women are held to be of equal worth and dignity. The problem with this model is that the differences between the genders are disregarded and the body is undervalued. *Gender polarity,* which found favor with Aristotle, claims that there are philosophical differences, but that man is, by nature, superior to woman. The danger with this model is that it disregards equality and over-values an aspect of the body of one of the genders. *Gender complementarity,* the third model, holds that there are real philosophical differences between man and woman, but that woman is not inferior to man. Until recent years, this model has often fallen into what Sr. Prudence Allen, RSM, calls "fractional sex complementarity." By this, she means that some philosophers have "sometimes divided masculine and feminine characteristics into parts so that one gender necessarily had one aspect and the other had the complement aspect." Fr. John Riccardo concurs, and explains the danger with this model is that the human being was understood to be fractional: both a man and a woman are required to make a single whole person. [25]

Corinthian   7

24   John Paul II, "Complementarity and Reciprocity between Women and Men," 2, in *The Genius of Women*, p. 24.
25   Riccardo, "Mutual Subordination of Husband and Wife," pp. 73-74.

epistemology: The branch of philosophy that studies the nature of knowledge, its presuppositions and foundations, and its extent and validity.

NOTES

The appropriate model for understanding the philosophical question regarding sex identity, Sr. Prudence Allen claims, is what she calls "integral sex complementarity." She explains: "A man or a woman as an individual has reason and intuition, understanding and sense, or universal and particular judgments. Each is a whole in respect to these **epistemological** categories. But, when a man and a woman interact in a relationship of complementarity, because some of the content of their consciousness is different due to their different relationships to maleness, femaleness, masculinity, and femininity, the interaction leads to something more. Using a mathematical metaphor, it could be said that fractional sex complementarity is expressed as $1/2 + 1/2 = 1$, while integral sex complementarity is expressed as $1 + 1 >> 3$." [26]

In giving themselves wholly to one another, husband and wife make themselves "responsible coworkers in the gift of life."[27] This responsibility involves equal and active collaboration by both husband and wife. Just as it would be contrary to self-giving love to reduce one's spouse to a mere object as a means to have children, it would be contrary to the same plan to "use" one's spouse as an object for one's own personal pleasure or gain. Both man and woman are called to participate actively in their most natural relationship, a "unity of the two," to which God has entrusted the work of procreation and family life. Because of their mutual complementarity, husbands and wives as fathers and mothers bring about different and complementary gifts, enriching all those in the family. The special communion of love between man and woman in marriage, which mirrors that of the interior life of the Trinity, is naturally love which gives life—life which is both biological and spiritual. It "enables each to experience their interpersonal and reciprocal relationship as a gift which enriches and which confers responsibility"[28] to both men and women.

In addition to having shared responsibility with men in procreating new life and nurturing life in the family, we also have a shared responsibility in caring for the earth and using its resources responsibly. Ultimately, these resources are not our own, but they belong to the One who has entrusted them to us. We are to be stewards of the gifts. We are also charged with the task of transforming the face of the earth, of creating and sustaining a culture of love and life. This task has been entrusted to women as much as men, who "help" one another to be fully human. In the collaboration of men and women, in a special way in the marriage relationship, and in every human friendship, the whole is greater

26   Sr. Prudence Allen, "Integral Sex Complementarity and the Theology of Communion," *Communio* 17 (Winter 1990): 523-544. Allen uses the word "gender" to include the word "sex" because the root of gender is in *gens*, and includes the meaning of engender and generation. It is also a way to overcome the mistaken division of sex (as biological) from gender (as psycho-social).
27   John Paul II, "Complementarity and Reciprocity between Women and Men," 2, in *The Genius of Women*, p. 24.
28   John Paul II, *Letter to Women*, 8, in *The Genius of Women*, p. 53.

NOTES

than the sum of the parts. The contribution of women is not to be underestimated by our late Holy Father. On behalf of the Church, he lauds the contribution of women "in the various sectors of society," stating that all these areas, as well as "nations, states and the progress of all humanity, are certainly deeply indebted to the contribution of women!"

DISCUSSION QUESTIONS

1. Does a woman need a man to be whole?

2. How does "integral sex complementarity" differ from former understandings of the relationship between men and women?

3. In Sr. Prudence Allen's model of "integral sex complementarity," what good comes from our mutual self-giving?

4. Who is our model of Love?

For Personal Meditation

What made you establish man in so great a dignity? Certainly your incalculable love by which you have looked on your creature in yourself! You are taken with love for her; for by love indeed you created her, by love you have given her a being capable of tasting your eternal good.

–St. Catherine of Siena [29]

NOTES

chapter 6

The Genius of Women

Progressive Woman *(Read the first paragraph of no. 9)*

At some time or another, many of us have witnessed some variation on this scene: A young college student is home for the weekend. As they sit around the dinner table, she informs her family she has an announcement to make. "After much consideration," she says, "I have finally declared my major." She pauses for a moment; then her wide grin declares the monumental word: "Ethics!" Around the table, heads tilt, eyebrows raise, the wrinkles of puzzlement replace hopeful smiles of eager expectation. In the silence hangs the question, "What on earth are you going to do with that?"

In a culture driven by Anglo-Saxon pragmatism, it is difficult to imagine putting effort into something that seems so "impractical." For many of us, it is difficult to imagine the purpose of doing something that does not have at its end something to be produced, manufactured, or sold. And while the value of scientific and technological advancements ought not to be ignored (since they are indeed important), these pursuits are but a *means* to an end, not the end themselves. They must always be put at the service of the person, who is an end in himself or herself.

Often, our product-driven culture has a hard time grasping why it would be worthwhile to spend time relishing the social sciences and the arts. Why study philosophy or theology? For the pursuit of truth. Why study music? For the sake of beauty. Why ethics? For the sake of goodness. Truth, beauty, and goodness are ends in and of themselves, for they are attributes of God himself who is Truth, Beauty, and the Ultimate Good. As the old joke teases, "In heaven, there will be no need of lawyers, for there will be no lawsuits. There will be no need of doctors, for there will be no sick people. There will be, however, plenty of poets, artists, and musicians, who will continuously point to the glory of God."

Without underrating the role of the positive sciences and technology in human progress, John Paul II reminds us that this is not "the only measure of progress, nor in fact is it the principal one. Much more important," he writes, "is *the social and ethical dimension*, which deals with human relations and spiritual values."[1] In his homily at the

Genius: Essential nature or spirit.

NOTES

Mass that opened the papal conclave, Cardinal Ratzinger—soon to become Pope Benedict XVI—addressed his brother cardinals and the faithful present in St. Peter's Basilica with this message: "All people desire to leave a lasting mark. But what endures? Money does not. Even buildings do not, nor books. After a certain time, longer or shorter, all these things disappear. The only thing that lasts forever is the human soul, the human person created by God for eternity."[2] The principal measures of progress, then, are those by which we love. "The fruit that endures," continues Cardinal Ratzinger, "is … all that we have sown in human souls: love, knowledge, a gesture capable of touching hearts, words that open the soul to joy in the Lord."[3]

Women have a gift for recognizing and living this profound truth. In the very essence of our being, we have a capacity for recognizing the value of persons over things and the primacy of being and relationship over having and doing. Exercising this gift from God, which is so vital to the future of humanity, is what John Paul II calls the *"genius of women."*

DISCUSSION QUESTIONS

1. What is the danger in valuing the "means" over the "end"?

2. Where do we see this danger realized in our modern world?

3. What lasts beyond this life?

4. How would your life look different if, at the end of each day, you measured your progress in life by the measurement of love? What would be at the top of your priority list?

---

2   Homily of His Eminence, Joseph Cardinal Ratzinger, Dean of the College of Cardinals, "Pro Eligendo Romano Pontifice" (18 April 2005); available from www.vatican.va/gpII/documents/homily-pro-eligendo-pontifice_20050418_en.html; Internet; accessed 12 November 2005.
3   Ibid.

The Feminine Genius

John Paul II wrote and spoke on the topic of the *"genius of women."* The term *genius* has many connotations. In the sense that John Paul II uses the term, it expresses *an essential nature or spirit*.[4] In other words, in recognizing the *"genius of women,"* he is honoring us for who we are and how we act in relation to other persons, for the very gift of womanhood that we bring to every area of society, to the family, and to the Church.

John Paul II drew upon several philosophical and theological sources as he developed an ontology of woman. One was the work of Edith Stein, the early twentieth-century philosopher who was recently canonized by John Paul II. Edith Stein was born in 1891 to a Jewish family in what is now Wroclaw, Poland. She converted from atheism to Catholicism while studying philosophy at a German university, and she continued her pursuit of an academic career as writer and lecturer on the nature and education of women. She went on to pursue a religious vocation to the Carmelite order, much to the dismay of her mother. She later took the name Sister Teresa Benedicta of the Cross. As a nun, she continued her intellectual work as a writer on philosophical and spiritual themes, including a study of St. John of the Cross and the metaphysics of finite and eternal being, until she was deported by the Nazis to Auschwitz in 1942. There, she was martyred in the Holocaust.

Stein, like St. Thomas Aquinas and Aristotle, acknowledged that there are traits unique to the human soul, abilities (or at least dispositional traits) that are shared by every member of the human species, male and female. Among these traits are rationality and the capacity for free choice. Aristotle had held that the human soul is like a stamp that, when united with the body, becomes individuated as a specific individual. Stein, in her early works, thought that a woman's soul had a unique formal identity when created by God that was joined to a female body. She extended the work of Aristotle, reasoning that because the body and the soul are so intimately united in the human person, the physical differences between men and women profoundly mark their personalities as the body is experienced in the psyche. She did not argue that biology is destiny, but rather, that a woman's body/soul unity has particular qualities that are (1) common to all women and (2) different from distinctively masculine traits, although women can be educated to express masculine traits. While maintaining a deep commitment to the freedom and individuality of each person, she was also committed to the existence of a

4   See the foreword to *The Genius of Women*, p. 13.

The word **ethos** is derived from the Greek ethos, meaning custom, character; the distinguishing character, sentiment, moral nature or guiding beliefs of a person, group or institution.

In *Mulierius Dignitatem*, John Paul II describes how *"woman is endowed with a particular capacity for accepting the human being in his concrete form"* (cf. no. 18). Thus, feminine presence in every aspect of society is part of the antidote for Marxist idealism which, as we saw in chapter one of this study, reduces man in his concrete form to something abstract.

NOTES

distinctly feminine **ethos**. The differences between women and men, then, are complementary and ought to be protected and celebrated, rather than ranked in a hierarchy of value, minimized, or lamented.

That women and men are not the same is a matter of common sense that we witness in our everyday lives. Philosopher Laura Garcia notes "[Stein's] thesis would be denied by many [old-line] feminists today, but probably not by anyone who has children of both genders. The differences between girls and boys appear early, and seem stubbornly resistant to manipulation by well-meaning politically correct parents … Nature has a way of asserting herself in unperturbed disregard for our theories."[5]

Among other gifts, woman has a remarkable capacity for empathy. Edith Stein wrote extensively about empathy in her doctoral dissertation. She described empathy as a clear awareness of another person, not simply of the *content* of his experience but of *his experience of that content*. In empathy, one takes the place of the other without becoming exactly identical to him. She "walks a mile in his shoes." Empathy means not merely understanding the experiences of the other, but in some sense *taking them on as* one's own.[6] This enriches our genius for friendship and for affective, cultural, and spiritual motherhood.

In his address "The Feminine Genius," John Paul II conveyed the Church's gratitude towards God and women for the gift of woman:

> Woman has a genius all her own which is vitally essential to both society and the Church. It is certainly not a question of comparing woman to man since it is obvious that they have fundamental dimensions and values in common. However, in man and in woman these acquire different strengths, interests, and emphases, and it is this very diversity which becomes a source of enrichment.

> In *Mulieris Dignitatem* I highlighted one aspect of feminine genius that I would like to stress today: *woman is endowed with a particular capacity for accepting the human being in his concrete form* (cf. no. 18). Even this singular feature which prepares her for motherhood, not only physically but also emotionally and spiritually, is inherent in the plan of God who entrusted the human being to woman in an altogether special way (cf. ibid., no. 30). The woman of course, as much as the man, must take care that her sensitivity does not succumb to the

5   Garcia, "The Role of Woman in Society."
6   Ibid.

temptation to possessive selfishness, and must put it at the service of authentic love. On these conditions she gives of her best, everywhere adding a touch of generosity, tenderness and joy of life.[7]

The "feminine genius" is a gift, one that is inherent to our very being that comes to fulfillment only if we receive it by cooperating with God's grace throughout our lifetimes. It is both a natural accompaniment to our potential for motherhood that is fully realized only through a deliberate choice and decision made on the part of each woman to bring it to full blossom. It cannot be reduced to a "feeling" of sensitivity that comes and goes, nor can it be reduced to a natural inclination that does not require a decision on our part. The "feminine genius" describes who we are, the essence of our nature which is endowed with a special capacity to call the world back to a "priority of love," which never reduces the person to an object, but recognizes his or her immeasurable dignity as a child of God created for infinite love and eternal life.

7   John Paul II, "The Feminine Genius," 2, in *The Genius of Women*, pp. 27-28.

If the Church was a body composed of different members, it couldn't lack the noblest of all: it must have a Heart burning with love. And I realized that this love alone was the true motive force which enabled the other members of the Church to act; if it ceased to function, the Apostles would forget to preach the gospel, the Martyrs would refuse to shed their blood. Love, in fact, is the vocation which includes all others; it's a universe of its own, compromising all time and space—it's eternal!

—*St. Thérèse of Liseux*
(see CCC 826)

NOTES

DISCUSSION QUESTIONS

1. What exactly is the "feminine genius"?

2. Where does it come from?

3. In her discourse on the feminine soul, Edith Stein wrote, "To cherish, guard, protect, nourish and advance growth is her natural, maternal yearning."[8] How do we see the "feminine genius" in young girls?

4. Where can the "genius of women" be put into practice?

5. Given your state in life, how can you put your "feminine genius" to work?

---

8   Edith Stein, "The Ethos of Women's Professions," in Edith Stein, *Collected Works*, v. 2: *Essays on Woman*, tr. Freda Mary Oben. Washington, DC: ICS Publications 1987, as cited by Garcia, "The Role of Woman in Society."

The Genius of Women at the Service of Love
(Read the second half of no. 9 and the first paragraph of no. 10)

Woman's special capacity for accepting the human being in his concrete form enables her to see persons beyond institutions and strategies, beyond political structures, social classes, and across cultures. This is a gift that she brings to the heart of the family, to political life, to social and economic spheres, to science and art, to culture and to every other area of society and the life of the Church. In this portion of the letter, John Paul II emphasizes the importance of social and ethical dimensions of progress. In doing so, he extends his appreciation to women who work in various areas extending well beyond the family: specifically, in education, healthcare, and working with the most needy and vulnerable of human life.

In his letter to us—which, we must not forget, is a letter addressed to each one of us, personally—John Paul II tells us that in working with the weakest and most defenseless, women exhibit a kind of "affective, cultural, and spiritual motherhood that has inestimable value for the development of individuals and the future of society."[9] All of us, whether or not we have ever carried a child in our wombs and whether we are married, single, or consecrated, are spiritual mothers whenever we give generously of ourselves to foster life in others.

Speaking of the "manifold, immense, although frequently silent, contribution of women in every area of human life"[10] John Paul II drew special attention to woman as teacher. He spoke of the "extremely positive" increasing presence of women in education as one which, he hoped, would lead to "a qualitative leap in the educational process itself."[11]

His hope, he wrote, was well-founded "if one considers the deep meaning of education, which cannot be reduced to the dry imparting of concepts but must aim at the full growth of man in all his dimensions. In this respect, how can we fail to understand the importance of the 'feminine genius'? It is also indispensable for the initial education in the family. Its 'educational' effect on the child begins when he is still in his mother's womb."[12]

"But the woman's role in the rest of the formational process is just as important," John Paul II continues. "She has a unique capacity to see the person as an individual, to understand his aspirations and needs with special insight, and she is able to face up to problems with deep involvement. The universal values themselves, which any sound education must always present, are offered by feminine

9   John Paul II, *Letter to Women*, 9.
10 John Paul II, "History Needs to Include Women's Contributions," 1, in *The Genius of Women*, pp. 29.
11 Ibid.
12 Ibid.

sensitivity in a tone complementary to that of man. Thus the whole educational process will certainly be enriched when men and women work together in training projects and institutions."[13]

"Investment in the care and education of girls as an equal right is a fundamental key to advancement of women," our Holy Father wrote in a letter to Mary Ann Glendon. He appealed to all educational services linked to the Catholic Church to "guarantee equal access for girls, to educate boys to a sense of women's dignity and worth, to provide additional possibilities for girls who have suffered disadvantage, and to identify and remedy the reasons which cause girls to drop out of education at an early age."[14]

Another area in which the "feminine genius" is particularly notable is the field of healthcare. Endowed with a special gift to see the person behind the disease, women nourish, protect and cure human life as physicians, nurses, therapists, surgeons, care takers and in a variety of other capacities. "How can I not think with gratitude of all the women who have worked and continue to work in the area of health care, not only in highly organized institutions, but also in very precarious circumstances, in the poorest countries of the world, thus demonstrating a spirit of service which not infrequently borders on martyrdom?" writes John Paul II. At the service of those most in need, these women preach the Gospel with their lives. Without words, they speak of Christ's merciful heart for the poor and the weak: As you did it to one of the least of my brethren, you did it to me.[15]

DISCUSSION QUESTIONS

1. What are some of the ways you have seen the "genius of women" working to build a culture of love?

2. Think of your favorite woman teacher. What was it about her that touched your life?

---

13 Ibid, pp. 28-29.
14 John Paul II, "Letter to Mary Ann Glendon and the Holy See's Delegation to the Fourth World Conference on Women (August 29, 1995)," in *The Genius of Women*, p. 60-61.
15 See Matthew 25:40.

Mary, Highest Expression of the Feminine Genius
(Read the rest of no. 10)

"The Church sees in Mary the highest expression of the 'feminine genius' and she finds in her a source of constant inspiration." Mary, the Mother of God, is the model of the whole Church and the archetype of every follower of Christ, man and woman. In her *fiat*, she humbly accepted the Lord's proposal, surrendering her flesh and blood, her body and soul, her entire being to God's will that she might give Life to the world.[16] In her vocation as wife and mother, she put herself at God's service and the service of his people in a *service of love*. She is the "only human person who eminently fulfills God's plan of love for humanity."[17]

If anyone in the history of humanity had reason to think of herself as better-than-thou, it was Mary. Having been redeemed by the saving merits of her Son, she was preserved from original sin at the moment of her conception.[18] And yet, she lived her privileged position as the Mother of the Redeemer with the utmost humility. She is invoked as the "Queen of heaven and earth" and hailed as we sing, "Salve, Regina!" which means, "Hail, Queen!"[19] *"For her, 'to reign' is 'to serve!' Her service is 'to reign'!"*[20]

In Mark 10:42-45, Jesus gives a stern warning to the apostles about how they are to lead. He tells them, "You know that those who are supposed to rule over the Gentiles lord it over them, and their great men exercise authority over them. But it shall not be so among you; but whoever would be great among you must be your servant, and whoever would be first among you must be slave of all. For the Son of Man also came not to be served but to serve, and to give his life as a ransom for many." Mary, in her maternal leadership, is the exemplar servant of God.

In making of herself a "sincere gift of self" to her Son, she has also become a gift for the sons and daughters of the whole human race, whether or not they ever recognize her as their mother. "For the family of God includes everyone: not just those who through baptism become God's adopted children, but in a certain sense all mankind, since Christ has redeemed all men and all women and offered them the possibility of becoming adopted sons and daughters of the eternal Father."[21] In fulfilling herself by a sincere gift of love, she has tread the path to our fulfillment, a path paved by self-giving love.

16 See *Lumen Gentium*, 53.
17 John Paul II, "Mary Shows Us God's Respect for Women (General Audience, November 29, 1995)," 2; Internet; accessed 15 November 2005. Hereafter John Paul II, General Audience, November 29, 1995.
18 See Pope Pius IX, *Ineffabilis Deus*.
19 For more on the Queenship of Mary, see Pope Pius XII, Papal Document on the Queenship of Mary *Ad Caeli Reginam* (October 11, 1954); Internet, available from www.vatican.va/holy_father/pius_xii/encyclicals/ documents/hf_p-xii_enc_11101954_ad-caeli-reginam_en.html, accessed 12 November 2005.
20 John Paul II, *Letter to Women*, 9.
21 John Paul II, "Holy Thursday Letter to Priests (April 7, 1995)," 4, in *The Genius of Women*, p. 67.

Mary abandoned herself entirely to the will of the God. In fidelity to her own vocation, she pointed to our *final goal* in life, union with her Son, our Lord. Her fidelity encourages us to remain faithful to our own vocations so as to obtain this union with our Lord, too. This goal provides meaning and direction for the earthly labors of both men and women alike.

Mary, the model of the New Feminism, is the highest expression of the feminine genius. "Mary is 'blessed among women'; however, every woman shares in some way in her sublime dignity in the divine plan."[22] John Paul II recognized her genius at the wedding at Cana: "John's Gospel offers us vivid detail of her personality when it tells how, in the busy atmosphere of a wedding feast, she alone realized that the wine was about to run out. And to avoid the couple's joy becoming embarrassment and awkwardness, she did not hesitate to ask Jesus for his first miracle. This is the 'genius' of woman! May Mary's thoughtful sensitivity, totally feminine and maternal, be the ideal mirror of all true femininity and motherhood!"[23]

DISCUSSION QUESTIONS

1. Why is Mary the "highest expression of the feminine genius"?

2. What is meant by the phrase, "For [Mary], 'to reign' is to serve!"?

3. What kind of a mother is Mary?

4. Read together the *Catechism*, 969-972. Do you depend on Mary's intercession? Do you strive to imitate her?

---

22 John Paul II, General Audience, November 29, 1995.
23 John Paul II, "The Feminine Genius," 3, in *The Genius of Women*, p. 28.

For Personal Meditation

Women first learn and then teach others that human relationships are authentic if they are open to accepting the other person: a person who is recognized and loved because of their dignity which comes from being a person and not from other considerations, such as usefulness, strength, intelligence, beauty, or health. This is a fundamental contribution, which the Church and humanity expect from women. And it is the indispensable prerequisite for an authentic cultural change.

–John Paul II, *Evangelium Vitae, 99*

NOTES

chapter 7

Service Signs

Dan Brown's best-selling and very misleading novel, *The Da Vinci Code*, has revived interest in the "secret love life" of Jesus. In the dramatic thriller, Brown "uncovers" one of the most massive conspiracies of all time: that the successors to the apostles have staged a two-thousand year cover-up of Jesus' love affair with one of his dearest followers. Brown comes to the rescue, enlightening his readers with newly uncovered "facts" from the Gnostic gospels which, he claims, have been purposefully hidden in the secret archives of the Vatican. (Brown must not have known that he or anyone else could have easily downloaded them on the Internet.) Among the most shocking of Brown's "revelations" is that the Holy Grail does not refer to the chalice Christ used at the Last Supper; but rather, to his lover, Mary Magdalene.[1]

In today's study, we will expose a truth that may come as shocking to Dan Brown and his fans: Jesus was indeed married! He was married in much more profound way than Dan Brown ever imagined. In this portion of the Holy Father's letter to us, he introduces the theme of the *sacramental **economy***; that is, the "economy of signs" that God freely chooses in order to become present in the midst of humanity.

We are all accustomed to signs and symbols: We see a green light, and we know we can drive ahead. We hear the siren of an ambulance, and we know to pull off to the side of the road. *Sacramental* signs, however, not only signify the thing they are representing, but they also are vehicles through which God actually gives his grace to us. Since all of reality is created by God, all of reality discloses something about who God is. A married couple discloses something about the love relationship between Christ and his Church. Likewise, the ministerial priesthood discloses something of Christ, the divine Bridegroom, who "first loved us"[2] and who gives us himself in the celebration of the Eucharist. Our participation in the Church and in a special way, the vows of a consecrated woman, discloses something of the gift of the Bride in response to the gift of the Bridegroom.

As we study the different vocations in the *sacramental economy*, we will be building upon the foundation that John Paul II laid for us last week, namely, that God has revealed to us in the

The Fathers of the Church distinguish between **theology** (*theologia*) and **economy** (*oikonomia*). "Theology" refers to the mystery of God's inmost life within the Blessed Trinity, while "economy" refers to all the works by which God reveals himself and communicates his life. Through the *oikonomia* the *theologia* is revealed to us; but conversely, the *theologia* illuminates the whole *oikonomia*. God's works reveal who he is in himself; the mystery of his inmost being enlightens our understanding of all his works. So it is, analogously, among human persons. A person discloses himself in his actions, and the better we know the person, the better we understand his actions.
–CCC 236

NOTES

1 See Dan Brown, *The Da Vinci Code* (New York: Doubleday, 2003).
2 Cf. 1 John 4:9

When you received the **Sacrament of Baptism**, the celebrant priest anointed your head with the sacred chrism and proclaimed these words over you, "God the Father of our Lord Jesus Christ has freed you from sin, given you new birth by water and the Holy Spirit, and welcomed you into his holy people. He now anoints you with the chrism of salvation. As Christ was anointed **Priest, Prophet, and King**, so may you live always as a member of his body, sharing everlasting life." On that day, you became a "new creation" (2 Cor 5:17) in Christ, cleansed "from sin in a new birth to innocence by water and Spirit" (cf. Acts 2:38; John 3:5). You have been adopted into God's family, made a "partaker of the divine nature" (2 Pet 1:4), a "member of Christ and coheir with him" (Gal 4:5-7; cf. 1 Cor 6:15; 12:27; Rom 8:17), and a "temple of the Holy Spirit" (cf. I Cor 6:19). You have been made a partaker in Christ's priestly, prophetic, and royal mission.[1]

NOTES

person of Mary precisely how he has invited all of us to share in his own life of radical, self-giving love. Abandoning herself completely to the truth of the living God, Mary is the model of faith and charity for all Christians, men and women alike.[3]

Christ, the Divine Bridegroom *(Read the first paragraph of no. 11)*

In his encyclical *On the Dignity of Woman, Mulieris Dignitatem,* John Paul II discusses the nature of the priesthood in the Church. Because this topic will be discussed in greater depth in ENDOW's *Mulieris Dignitatem* study, we will focus our discussion on a few main points that will help us understand this *sacramental sign* as one of the ways God reveals himself and his relationship to us.

Christ and the Common Priesthood

The Second Vatican Council, in the fifth chapter of *Lumen Gentium,* renewed the Church's awareness about the universality of the priesthood. In the New Covenant, there is only one sacrifice and only one priest—Christ. *All the baptized*—both men and women—*share in the one priesthood of Christ* inasmuch as we 1) present our bodies as a living sacrifice, whole and acceptable to God (cf. Rom 12:1), 2) give witness to Christ in every place, and 3) give an explanation to anyone who asks the reason for the hope in eternal life that is in us (cf. 1 Pt 3:15). "Universal participation in Christ's sacrifice, in which the Redeemer has offered to the Father the whole world and humanity in particular, brings it about that all in the Church are 'a kingdom of priests' (Rev 5:10; cf. 1 Pt. 2:9), who not only share in the priestly mission but also in the prophetic and kingly mission of Christ the Messiah."[4] Every single baptized person shares in the one priesthood of Christ. This is the "common priesthood" of which John Paul II speaks in *Letter to Women* 11. To participate in the common priesthood of Christ means that we are called to respond to the one priesthood of Christ by making of ourselves a gift to God and a gift to others. No matter what our vocation, *this is to be our life.* This is the universal call to holiness, which is the aim of the Christian life.

When we—as baptized men and women—participate in the one priesthood of Christ, we also participate in the "organic unity" of the Bride of Christ, the Church, with the divine Bridegroom, Christ himself. The Church is united to her Bridegroom in that she lives his life, she shares in his threefold mission (as priest, prophet,

1   *CCC,* 1217-1284, especially 1265.

3   See *Lumen Gentium,* 53.
4   John Paul II, *Mulieris Dignitatem,* 27.

and king), and she is united in such a manner as to respond with a "sincere gift" of self to the inexpressible gift of the love of the Bridegroom, the Redeemer of the world. "In the context of this great mystery of Christ and the Church, all are called to respond—as a bride—with the gift of our lives to the inexpressible gift of the love of Christ, who alone, as the redeemer of the world, is the Church's Bridegroom. The 'royal priesthood,' which is universal, at the same time expresses the gift of the Bride."[5]

The relationship between Christ and the Church, then, is a spousal relationship. Jesus is the Bridegroom. The Church—which the baptized, both men and women—is the Bride.[6] Each of us individually and all of us communally are called to enter into a spousal relationship with our Lord and Bridegroom. The relationship between Christ and the Church is analogous to the relationship between a husband and a wife, but not to the distorted view of marriage which, as a result of sin, is characterized by domination and servitude; rather, it is analogous to the relationship that God intended for spouses from the beginning, as we studied in Genesis 1 and 2, a relationship characterized by a generous gift of self.

In last week's study, we encountered our Holy Father's writings on the "genius" of Mary, the highest expression of the "feminine genius." She is the prototype, the exemplar for all of us who have been baptized into the common priesthood, because she, the "Queen of heaven and earth,"[7] understood that *to reign is to serve!*

5 Ibid.
6 Among the many Scriptural passages that reveal this truth, John Paul II points in particular to Matthew 9:15; John 3:29; 2 Corinthians 11:2; and Ephesians 5:25, which all refer to Jesus as the Bridegroom. 2 Corinthians 11:2; Ephesians 5:25-27,31-32; and Revelation 19:7 and 21:9 refer to the Church as the Bride.
7 For more on the Queenship of Mary, see Pope Pius XII, Papal Document on the Queenship of Mary *Ad Caeli Reginam* (October 11, 1954); Internet, available from www.vatican.va/holy_father/pius_xii/encyclicals/ documents/hf_p-xii_enc_11101954_ad-caeli-reginam_en.html, accessed 12 November 2005.

Christ, high priest and unique mediator, has made of the Church 'a kingdom, priests for his God and Father.' The faithful exercise their baptismal priesthood through their participation, each according to his own vocation, in Christ's mission as priest, prophet and king.

–CCC 1546

NOTES

Christ and the Ministerial Priesthood

Some in the common priesthood are called to the particular service of the ministerial priesthood. John Paul II emphatically repeated that the ministerial priesthood is not a career and it is not about power. It's about service. That is *the* purpose of the vocation. In an address to a group of American bishops, John Paul II underscored, "The New Testament witness and the constant tradition of the Church remind us that the ministerial priesthood cannot be understood in sociological or political categories, as a matter of exercising 'power' within the community. The priesthood of Holy Orders must be understood theologically, as one form of service in and for the Church."[8]

"Although the Church possesses a 'hierarchical' structure," writes John Paul II, "nevertheless this structure is totally ordered to the holiness of Christ's members. And holiness is measured according to the 'great mystery' in which the bride responds with the gift of love to the gift of the bridegroom."[9] The *Catechism* explains, "[T]he ministerial priesthood is at the service of the common priesthood. It is directed at the unfolding of the baptismal grace of all Christians. The ministerial priesthood is a *means* by which Christ unceasingly builds up and leads his Church."[10] Its purpose is to help others grow in holiness and to find fulfillment as people created in the image and likeness of God. It must be motivated by love.

We recall Jesus' stern warning to his Apostles that we read last week in Mark 10:42-45, in which he instructed these men who would become the first to participate in his ministerial priesthood on how they were to lead, reminding them that "whoever would be first among you must be slave of all." The night before he died, Christ instituted the Sacrament of the Eucharist and entrusted the ministerial priesthood to the Apostles. At that "Last Supper," he, the Savior of the World, stooped to wash the feet of those Apostles, saying, "Do you know what I have done to you? You call me Teacher and Lord; and you are right, for so I am. If I then, your Lord and Teacher, have washed your feet, you also ought to wash one another's feet. For I have given you an example, that you also should do as I have done to you" (Jn 13:12-15). The next day, Jesus laid down his life on the Cross out of love for his Bride. This is how those who have been called to the ministerial priesthood are called to serve.

Holy Orders, by which one is ordained to the ministerial priesthood, is a **sacrament**. In every sacrament three things are necessary: an

8   See John Paul II, "Address of John Paul II to the bishops from the states of Michigan and Ohio (U.S.A.) on their 'Ad Limina' visit (21 May 1998);" Internet, available from http://www.vatican.va/holy_father/john_paul_ii/speeches/1998/may/documents/hf_jp-ii_spe_19980521_ad-limina-usa_en.html, accessed 16 January 2006.
9   John Paul II, *Mulieris Dignitatem*, 27.
10 *CCC* 1547.

outward sign, an inward grace, and divine institution. The Sacrament of Holy Orders is a *vocation* which, as we recall from our discussion of Mary's vocation from our second week, is a calling or an invitation. It is not something somebody has a *right* to; but rather, it is a gift, initiated by God, and freely received by the one being called. Jesus, in the Gospel of John, tells his disciples, "You did not chose me, but I chose you" (Jn 15:16). As a calling, a vocation involves dialogue between two. It must be expressed by both partners. In a vocation to marriage, both the man and the woman must express their will to be married. Likewise, in a vocation to the ministerial priesthood, both the priestly candidate and his Bride, the Church, must consent to be wed.[11]

While Jesus called many women to follow him, he did not call any of them to the group he entrusted with the task of being an "'icon of his countenance as 'shepherd' and 'bridegroom' of the Church through the exercise of the ministerial priesthood."[12] Based on the foundation of the example and attitude of her Lord, the practice of the Apostles, and the constant Tradition of the Church, John Paul II reaffirmed that "The Church, in fidelity to the example of the Lord, *does not consider herself authorized* to admit women to the ministerial priesthood."[13]

Of the three-part foundation mentioned above, the first—the example and attitude of Christ—is most important. Could it have been that Jesus was simply conditioned by the culture in which he lived, a culture that would not have tolerated women priests? If the Christ's behavior towards women surrendered in conformity to those of the culture in which he lived, perhaps this objection would deserve more attention. However, Jesus' own actions reveal that he had little regard for the opinions of others in the community. He repeatedly interacted with women in a way entirely foreign and even contrary to the customs of the time. We see it in his interaction with the woman at the well in John 4, in his interaction with the Samaritan woman in Matthew 9, and in his interaction with the prostitute in Luke 7. He recognized divorce and adultery, not only as an injustice to man, but also to woman. His actions were oriented towards the correction and chastisement of those who failed to see that God had created both men and women in his own image and likeness, that all are called to participate in the dignity of the divine life, and that an offense against the human person—male or female—is an offense against God.[14]

A **sacrament** is "an efficacious sign of grace, instituted by Christ and entrusted to the Church, by which divine life is dispensed to us."
–CCC 1131

NOTES

11 See *CCC* 1578. In this case, it is the bishop who accepts the candidate for orders following the ordinate rites he has received.
12 John Paul II, *Letter to Women*, 11.
13 John Paul II, Apostolic Letter On Reserving Priestly Ordination to Men Alone, *Ordinatio Sacerdotalis* (May 22, 1984), 2, quoting an affirmation from the Sacred Congregation for the Doctrine of the Faith, Declaration on the Question of the Admission of Women to the Ministerial Priesthood, *Inter Insigniores*, 15 (October 15, 1976), emphasis added.
14 See Riccardo, "Why an All-Male Priesthood?"

When the Church states that she, "in fidelity to the example of the Lord, does not consider herself authorized to admit women to the ministerial priesthood,"[15] it is not a claim to obstinacy. The Church is acknowledging her limits. She considers her Lord's example to be binding upon her.[16]

So, then, why would Jesus have reserved the ministerial priesthood to men alone? Is it because men are superior to women? Given all we have studied here, we can wholeheartedly reject this possibility. Is it because men reveal God more than women? Genesis 1 and 2 made it clear that this is not the case. Is it because men are more naturally equipped to preach? Few would argue that women lack such linguistic skills, so that cannot be it. Is it that only men make good leaders? The witness of incredible women saints and Doctors of the Church attest to the ridiculousness of that assertion. Are men more intelligent than women? No. Are they more suited for holiness? No, that's for everyone. Is it that men are more adept in people skills? If anything, the reverse would be true.[17] Why, then, does the Church continue to reserve the ministerial priesthood for men alone?

"If a reason is to be sought as to why Jesus reserved admission to the ministerial priesthood to men, it can be discovered in the fact that the priest represents Christ himself in his relationship to the Church. Now," John Paul continues, "this relationship is spousal in nature: Christ is the Bridegroom, the Church is the Bride."[18] We experience the spousal relationship between Christ and his Bride most clearly and unambiguously in the Sacrament of the Eucharist, which, as Vatican II reminds us, is "the source and summit of the whole Christian life."[19] In it, we are united in our bodies; we are made one flesh with Christ, the divine Bridegroom. This sacrament, which Christ linked to the priestly service of the apostles, is the essence of the priesthood. As he consecrates the Eucharist, the priest does not act in his own name, but represents Christ, who acts through him. It is the Eucharist, above all, that expresses the redemptive act of the Bridegroom to his Church, the Bride.[20]

The representation is a two-sided reality, in which the one represented has been authorized by the one he represents to make present something of the latter's dignity, but without being able to claim any of that superiority or dignity for himself.

15 *Inter Insigniores*, 15.
16 See Riccardo, "Why an All-Male Priesthood?"
17 Ibid.
18 John Paul II, General Audience, July 27, 1994.
19 Vatican II, *Lumen Gentium*, 11.
20 Ibid.

This is not to say that God is male. As the *Catechism* makes clear, "God is pure spirit in which there is no place for the difference between sexes," so God is neither male nor female. [21] It is also not to say that a woman cannot represent Christ—she does, by virtue of her Baptism. The same can be said of a man who has not received the Sacrament of Holy Orders. It is to say that there is something special about the representation of Christ in the Eucharist, the essence of the priesthood which sacramentally makes present again—here and now—the Bridegroom's gift of himself to the Bride.[22]

In his letter of thanksgiving and solidarity, John Paul II emphasizes, as he did so frequently in his pontificate, that "this in no way detracts from the role of women, or for that matter from the role of the other members of the Church who are not ordained to the sacred ministry, since all share equally in the dignity proper to the 'common priesthood' based on Baptism." It would in fact be a grave injustice and a denial of rights if the Church taught that ordained priests were the greatest in the Church, or that only ordained priests have a complete relationship with God, or that only priests can reach the goal of the Christian life, which is holiness. The Church teaches none of these. The ministerial priesthood is "an expression ... of service."[23] As we will see in our next section, woman also has a unique and fundamental role in the "economy of signs."

21 See *CCC* 370.
22 See Riccardo, "Why an All-Male Priesthood?"
23 John Paul II, "Holy Thursday Letter to Priests (April 7, 1995)," 7, in *The Genius of Women*, p. 71.

NOTES

DISCUSSION QUESTIONS

1. Who is the one priest in the New Covenant?

2. How do we, the baptized, participate in the "common priesthood" of Christ?

3. What is Christ's relationship with his Church?

4. How does he love her?

5. How does Christ, the divine Bridegroom, give himself to us today?

6. Who is the Source of the Sacraments?

The Church, the Bride in the Image of Mary
(Read the second paragraph of no. 11)

All those who are embraced by the communion of the Church are disciples. "That means," explains papal biographer George Weigel, "that everyone in the Church is formed in the image of a woman: Mary, the mother of Jesus, the first of disciples and thus the 'Mother of the Church.'"[24] Just as all are called to be "sons" in "the Son," we are all called to be "brides" in "the Bride."

Weigel explains the significance of an understanding of the Church formed in the Image of Mary:

> Every year the Pope meets with the senior members of the Roman Curia, the Church's central bureaucracy, for an exchange of Christmas greetings. It's a formal occasion, rather far removed from the typical office Christmas party. Popes traditionally use the opportunity to review the year just past and suggest directions for the year ahead. On December 22, 1987, Pope John Paul II made this the occasion to drop something of a theological bombshell.
>
> For some years, Catholic theologians had speculated about different 'profiles,' or 'images' of the Church, drawn from New Testament personalities. The missionary Church, the Church of proclamation, is formed in the image of the apostle Paul, the greater preacher to the Gentiles. The Church of contemplation is formed in the image of the apostle John, who rested his head on Christ's breast at the Last Supper. The Church of office and jurisdiction is formed in the image of Peter, the apostle to whom Christ gave the keys of the kingdom of heaven. All of these images are in play in the Church all the time. Yet, in a Church accustomed for centuries to thinking of itself primarily in institutional terms, the Church formed in the image of Peter's authority and office has long seemed to take priority over all the rest.
>
> Not so, suggested John Paul II … Mary was the first disciple, because Mary's 'yes' to the angel's message had made possible the incarnation of the Son of God. The Church is the extension of Christ and his mission in history; in the image made famous by Pope Pius XII, the Church is the "Mystical Body of Christ." Mary's Assumption into heaven was a preview of what awaits all those whom Christ will save. For all these reasons,

John Paul proposed that Mary provides a defining profile of what the Church is, of how the men and women of the Church should live, and of what the eternal destiny of disciples will be.

This understanding of Mary and the Church challenges the institutional way in which many churchmen (and many Catholic laity) are used to thinking about themselves and their community. The 'Marian profile,' John Paul said, is even 'more … fundamental' in Catholicism than the 'Petrine profile.' Though the two cannot be divided, the 'Marian Church,' the Church formed in the image of a woman and her discipleship, precedes, makes possible, and indeed makes sense of the 'Petrine Church,' the Church of office and authority formed in the image of Peter. The Petrine Church, the Pope continued, has no other purpose 'except to form the Church in line with the ideal of sanctity already programmed and prefigured in Mary.' John Paul argued that these two profiles were complementary, not in tension. He also insisted that the 'Marian profile is … pre-eminent' and carried within it a richer meaning for every Christian's vocation.[25]

The implications of this are not slight for the dignity and "role" of every woman. For "there is present in the 'womanhood' of a woman who believes, and especially in a woman who is 'consecrated,' a kind of inherent 'prophecy' (cf. *Mulieris Dignitatem*, 29), a powerfully evocative symbolism, a highly significant 'iconic character,' which finds its full realization in Mary and which also aptly expresses the very essence of the Church as a community consecrated with the integrity of a 'virgin' heart to become the 'bride' of Christ and 'mother' of believers." By virtue of who we are as women and through the fulfillment of our vocations, we become icons of the "very essence of the Church." It is the Bridegroom who loves. The bride is loved: it is she who receives love, in order to love in return.[26]

25 Weigel, *The Truth of Catholicism*, pp. 45-46. See also John Paul II, "Annual Address to the Roman Curia," in *L'Osservatore Romano*, English Weekly Edition, January 11, 1988, pp. 6-8 and John Paul II, *Mulieris Dignitatem*, 27, including endnote 55.
26 John Paul II, *Mulieris Dignitatem*, 29.

DISCUSSION QUESTIONS

1. Why is the "Marian profile" of the Church antecedent to the 'Petrine profile'?

2. In the *economy of signs*, how do women make manifest to the world the "very essence of the Church"? In other words, how does a bride respond to her Bridegroom?

3. What are some practical ways in which we can strive to imitate Mary, the model of the bride?

In the history of the Church, some ecstatics have shared in the suffering of Christ through the **stigmata**, wherein the wounds of the Passion of Christ manifest themselves on the person's hands, feet, side and brow.

NOTES

The Feminine Genius in the Church
(Read the fourth paragraph of no. 11)

Throughout the two-thousand-year history of the Church, there have been numerous women saints, martyrs, and famous mystics who have followed Mary in putting their *feminine genius* to work at the service of Christ and the Church, leaving "an impressive and beneficial mark in history." In our study, we have encountered a few of these great women: Maria Montessori, who made the 'vital discovery' of the child and conceived of an original form of education on that basis; and St. Teresa Benedicta of the Cross (Edith Stein), the brilliant philosopher who converted to Catholicism and was martyred during the Holocaust.

The Holy Father also draws our attention to two Doctors of the Church "who have distinguished themselves in the Church's history by their holiness and hardworking ingenuity,"[27] namely, St. Catherine of Siena and St. Teresa of Avila.

St. Catherine (1347-1380) was the 25th child of a wool dyer in northern Italy. A mystic and visionary, St. Catherine was one of the most brilliant theological minds of her day, although she never had any formal education. In 1375 she received the **stigmata**, which was visible only after her death. She was so persuasive that she convinced the Pope to go back to Rome from Avignon, France. When she died she was endeavoring to heal the division in the Church that resulted from the Great Western Schism.[28] In a simple phrase, St. Catherine of Siena shared a secret for how to put the "feminine genius" at the service of love: "Be who you are and you will set the world ablaze."

Another example of the work of the "genius of woman" in the Church is St. Teresa of Avila (1515-1582), a Carmelite nun, who was not foreign to difficulties. She suffered many hardships, including family troubles, malaria, struggles in prayer, and embarrassing seizures. She complained, "Dear Lord, if this is how you treat your friends, it's no wonder you have so few of them!" Yet, through it all, she remained faithful. She contributed to the renewal of the entire ecclesiastical community and wrote outstanding works on asceticism and mysticism. Her spiritual teachings are a guide to a life in union with God.[29]

Discussing the contribution of women in the Church, John Paul II asks, "And how can we overlook the many women, inspired by faith, who were responsible for initiatives of extraordinary social

27 John Paul II, "Woman's Role in the Church," 1, in *The Genius of Women*, p. 35.
28 See "Saints and Angels: St. Catherine of Siena;" Internet, available from http://www.catholic.org/saints/, accessed 1 September 2005.
29 Ibid.

importance, especially in serving the poorest of the poor?" When John Paul II wrote these words in 1995, perhaps he was thinking of Blessed Mother Teresa of Calcutta in her simple white habit with three blue stripes, whose radiant love was not without sacrifice. She encouraged her Sisters of Charity to "love until it hurts and keep loving until it hurts no more." How easy it is to give up when it hurts and never experience the joy of loving until it hurts no more! In her book, *A Simple Path*, she wrote, "You must give what will cost you something. This, then, is giving not just what you can live without but what you can't live without or don't want to live without, something you really like. Then your gift becomes a sacrifice, which will have value before God. Any sacrifice is useful if it is done out of love."[30] Making the bed can be a useful sacrifice if done out of love. Cooking dinner can be useful if done out of love. Late night studying can be a useful sacrifice if done out of love. Leaving the sugar out of your coffee can be a useful sacrifice if done out of love. Her commitment to "ordinary acts with extraordinary love," made Mother Teresa one of the most influential women of the 20th century.

In a Sunday Angelus address, the Holy Father made an appeal "to the whole Church community to be willing to foster feminine participation in every way in its internal life," noting that "the Church is increasingly aware of the need for enhancing their role."[31] A 1987 Synod on the Laity expressed precisely this need and asked that "without discrimination women should be participants in the life of the Church, and also in consultation and the process of coming to decisions' (*Propositio* 47; cf. *Christifideles Laici*, no. 51)." "This is certainly not a new commitment," adds John Paul II, "since it is inspired by the example of Christ himself. Although he chose men as his apostles—a choice which remains normative for their successors—nevertheless, he involved women in the cause of his kingdom; indeed, he wanted them to be the first witnesses and heralds of his resurrection."[32]

There is ample room for feminine participation in the Church. John Paul II names a few ways to do this, including "theological teaching, the forms of liturgical ministry permitted, including service at the altar, pastoral and administrative councils, diocesan synods and particular councils, various ecclesial institutions, curias, and ecclesiastical tribunals, many pastoral activities, including new forms of participation in the care of parishes when there is a shortage of clergy, except for those tasks that belong properly to the priest. Who

30 Mother Teresa, *A Simple Path* (New York: Ballantine Books, 1995), p. 99.
31 John Paul II, "Woman's Role in the Church (September 3, 1995)," 1, in *The Genius of Women*, p. 35.
32 Ibid. p. 35-36.

NOTES

can imagine," he asks, "the great advantages to pastoral care and the new beauty that the Church's face will assume, when the feminine genius is fully involved in the various areas of her life?"[33]

Discussion Questions

1. Who is your favorite woman saint? Why? How did she give the gift of her feminine genius in love to Christ and the Church?

2. Where do you think Christ might be inviting you to give of your "feminine genius" at the service of the Church?

For Personal Meditation

Be who you are and you will set the world ablaze.

–St. Catherine of Siena

33 John Paul II "Woman's Role in the Church" 2. *The Genius of Women*, pp.s. 35-36.

chapter 8

The Calling

Eight weeks ago, we received a special letter. It was as though we had walked to our mailboxes to pick up the daily mail, and as we flipped through the stack of bills and greetings from friends, we noticed an unusual envelope with a Vatican airmail stamp addressed with unfamiliar handwriting. Yes, that was our name scrawled out on the front of the envelope. As we flipped it over, revealing a wax seal imprinted with John Paul II's papal crest with its predominant Marian "M" standing beneath the foot of the cross, it became apparent that this was no ordinary greeting. Curiously, we broke the seal to see what was inside.

"I greet you all most cordially, women throughout the world!" the letter began. He continued, as if to say, "My dear sister, you have been on my mind and heart a lot lately. I was wondering if you knew how precious you are to God, to the Church, and to the world. I know you are too often underestimated, underappreciated and unrecognized, so I am writing you this letter to offer my sincere gratitude to you for the many ways you use your gifts to enrich all of humanity! I am giving thanks to the Almighty God for the gift of you. He loves you so much and has created you for an incredible purpose. Too often, your special dignity, rights and purpose have not been recognized. If any of those who stood in the way of your full development are members of the Church, I am truly sorry and humbly ask for your forgiveness. Throughout history, women have encountered many obstacles to their full development, and these obstacles desperately need to be removed. The women's liberation movement has made many positive strides towards building a society where you can truly be yourselves, yet its work remains incomplete. I am afraid that our culture has lost touch with what really matters. It has become overly concerned with efficiency and productivity, and humans are valued for what they can do, how they look, or how useful they are. What is needed is a 'prophetic voice' to call the world back to a 'priority of love' which never reduces the person to an object. You, by virtue of your womanhood, have this special gift, and this gift is essential to building a more humane civilization. You, personally, have a unique mission, a special invitation from God, to share in his own divine life at the service of life and love. That is why I am appealing in a particular way to states and institutions throughout the world to open themselves to the influence of your feminine genius, to recognize and foster your full development as a woman. At the same time, I am inviting you, appealing to you, to put your 'feminine genius' to work for the sake of humanity to transform the 'culture of death' into a 'culture of life.'"[1]

And as we close his letter and slide it back into its envelope, our Holy Father's heartfelt appeal echoes in our hearts. He wrote this letter on the eve of the UN Conference on the Status of Women in Beijing in 1995, but his words resonate with remarkable relevance today. A worldview which reduces people to objects to be used slithers through the halls of our hospitals, the corridors of our universities, and through the television screen in our homes. Our Holy Father's letter has not only reminded of us who we are and the incredible gifts we have been given as women, it has also given us impetus to rejoice for the gift of the "feminine genius" and has emboldened us to live it anew.

1   See John Paul II, *Evangelium Vitae*, 99.

The "Genius of Women" at the Service of Others
(Read no. 12)

"The journey of [women's liberation] must go on!" the Holy Father has written us.[2] But it will involve more than a simple "condemnation of discrimination and injustices, necessary though this may be."[3] It demands more than criticizing the shortcomings of the women's liberation movement in the past. As someone once put it, "You do not win an argument with an argument. You win an argument with truth."[4] If solutions to problems facing women are to be "honest and permanent" they must be based on "the *recognition of the inherent, inalienable dignity of women*, and the importance of women's presence and participation in all aspects of social life."[5] The New Feminism must be a proclamation of "God's plan in a positive way so that a culture may develop that respects and welcomes 'femininity.'"[6]

The truth about the intrinsic dignity of the human person is recognizable through "the use of reason itself, which is able to understand the law of God written in the heart of every human being."[7] The revealed word of God in the Sacred Scriptures and Apostolic Tradition enable us to grasp the anthropological foundation of the dignity of women. God, in his infinite love and generosity has freely chosen to create us out of nothing. We are simply breathing right now because He has given us life. He has formed us in his own "image and likeness" (cf. Gn 1:26-28) and has called us to share in a life which far exceeds the temporal dimension. He has called us into his very own divine life,[8] a life of perpetual, self-giving love. This is the purpose for which we have been created. This is the destiny of every human person. We will only find fulfillment in making of ourselves a "sincere gift" to him and to others.[9]

Having been created in the "image and likeness" of God and destined for no less than eternal life, women, like men, share in a dignity infinitely more precious than the finest diamond or rarest pearl. Therefore, writes John Paul II, women have "a right to insist that [our] dignity be respected. At the same time, [we] have the duty to work for the promotion of the dignity of all persons, men as well as women."[10] And, as John Paul II reminds us, there is still a "need to achieve *real equality* in every area: equal pay for equal work, protection for working mothers, fairness in career advancement, equality for spouses with regard to family rights, and the recognition

2   John Paul II, Letter to Women, 6, in *The Genius of Women*, p. 51.
3   Ibid.
4   Fr. John Riccardo, speech given at "Catholics in the Public Square," St. John Center for Youth and Family in Plymouth, Michigan, 29 April 2003.
5   John Paul II, "Welcome to Gertrude Mongella," 2, in *The Genius of Women*, p. 38.
6   John Paul II, *Culture Must Respect Femininity*," 1, in *The Genius of Women*, p. 21, emphasis added.
7   John Paul II, *Letter to Women*, 6.
8   See 2 Peter 1: 4.
9   Vatican II, *Gaudium et Spes*, 24.
10 John Paul II, "World Day of Peace Message," 11, in *The Genius of Women*, p. 17.

of everything that is part of the rights and duties of citizens in a democratic state."[11]

Real equality is not only a "matter of justice, but also of necessity."[12] This is because women are endowed with a special capacity for accepting the person in his concrete form. We have a knack for placing *persons* above *things* and valuing *being and relationship* over *having and doing*. Our Holy Father writes, "Perhaps more than men, women acknowledge the person, because they see persons with their hearts. They see them independently of various ideological or political systems. They see others in their greatness and limitations; they try to go out to them and *help them*."[13] Our "feminine genius" is gift from our Creator. It is a gift to be given. By giving ourselves to others *each day*, writes John Paul II, we fulfill our deepest vocation. Because of our capacity to make room for another, a "greater presence of women in society will prove most valuable," he writes, for it will help to "manifest the contradictions present when society is organized solely according to the criteria of efficiency and productivity, and it will force systems to be redesigned in a way which favors the processes of humanization which mark the 'civilization of love.'"[14]

John Paul II has called upon states and institutions, and the United Nations in particular, to "bring out the full truth about women"[15] and to protect and celebrate those special differences and gifts that enable women to contribute what men cannot, rather than to deny them or eliminate them. The wounds of concupiscence have given rise to cultures which often ignore and, in some places, even condone the exploitation and domination of women. In the effort to combat exploitation and discrimination, some have attempted to deny complementary differences between men and women, but this is likely to lead to a further offense against women, for we will end up being measured according to a male norm, as though men are the "gold standard" and women are imperfect men. Such denial of our differences cannot help but be accompanied by a disregard for the greatness and distinctiveness that belongs to women.[16]

It is precisely because women are *not the same as men* that the contribution of women in society is so important. From the very beginning, as revealed in the book of Genesis, woman is a "helpmate" for man. Far from being a pejorative or demeaning role, the "help"

11 John Paul II, *Letter to Women*, 4.
12 Ibid.
13 John Paul II, *Letter to Women*, 12.
14 John Paul II, *Letter to Women*, 4.
15 John Paul II, *Letter to Women*, 12.
16 Ibid.

that woman gives to man is not "unilateral" but mutual.[17] It is more than her "help" in the self-giving act of procreation. It is more than her role as joint steward over the earth. As one theologian put it, she helps him "to be 'human.'"[18] Humanity was not complete until the moment of her creation, and humanity will be impoverished without her contribution today.

DISCUSSION QUESTIONS

1. Think back to eight weeks ago when we first opened John Paul II's *Letter to Women*. What did you expect to read?

2. How has your understanding of the dignity of woman deepened over the course of this study?

3. Have there been any surprises?

4. What portion of the letter has spoken to your heart the most?

5. Why is it necessary that the New Feminism consist in a positive campaign, based on the dignity of woman and her special feminine genius?

---

17 John Paul II, "Complementarity and Reciprocity between Women and Men," 1, in *The Genius of Women*, p. 24.
18 Francis Martin, manuscript on the biblical theology of marriage and family in the Old Testament. In Riccardo, "Mutual Subordination of Husband and Wife," p. 52.

6. In the third week of our study, John Paul II spoke of the great "debt" that humanity owes to women. "Yet how many women have and continue to be valued more for their physical appearance than for their skill, their professionalism, their intellectual abilities, their deep sensitivity; in a word, the very dignity of their being?"[19] Think of one way that you can communicate this message to the younger women in your life.

7. What are some ways you have seen women make the world more worthy of humanity?

The Treasure of Womanhood

In his letter to us, the Holy Father invites *ecclesial communities* to join him in making the year "an occasion of heartfelt thanksgiving to the Creator and Redeemer of the world for the gift of *this great treasure* which is womanhood. In all its expressions," he writes, "womanhood is part of the essential heritage of mankind and of the Church herself."[20] Women bring the riches of their femininity into the heart of the family, the Church, and the world.

In his Exhortation on *The Role of the Family in the Modern World*, John Paul wrote, "The future of the world and the Church passes through the family."[21] When we consider the role of women in transforming the culture, we must bear in mind, as Laura Garcia reminds us, that "devoting oneself to home and family on a full-time basis is itself a public witness, and a very important one."[22] She continues, "Focusing one's energies in this way on making the home a warm and welcoming environment and helping children to reach their potential, to find God and to find themselves, flies right in the face of the assumptions of the consumer culture."[23] In an earlier part of his letter to us, John Paul II acknowledges that "much remains to be done to prevent discrimination against those who have chosen to be wives and mothers."[24] He invites us to spread the message that women should not be "made to feel guilty for wanting to remain in the home and nurture and care for [their] children. A mother's presence in the family, so critical to the stability and growth of that basic unit of society, should instead be recognized, applauded and supported in every possible way."[25] At the same time, "husbands and fathers" are called "to their family responsibilities."[26] With the gift of motherhood, she is appointed "guardian of life."[27] Mothers, you become "God's own smile upon the newborn child, the one who guides your child's first steps, who helps it grow, and who is the anchor as the child makes its way along the journey of life."[28] "Parenthood—even though it belongs to both—is realized much more fully in the woman, especially in the prenatal period. It is the woman who 'pays' directly for this shared generation, which literally absorbs the energies of her body and soul. It is therefore necessary that the man be fully aware that in their shared parenthood he owes a special debt to women."[29]

20 John Paul II, *Letter to Women*, 12.
21 John Paul II, Post-Synodal Exhortation on The Role of the Family in the Modern World Familiaris Consortio (Boston: Daughters of St. Paul, 1981), 75.
22 Laura Garcia, "The Role of Woman in Society."
23 Ibid.
24 John Paul II, *Letter to Women*, 4.
25 John Paul II, "Welcome to Gertrude Mongella," 3, in *The Genius of Women*, p. 39.
26 Ibid.
27 John Paul II, "The Vocation to Motherhood," 2, in *The Genius of Women*, p. 26.
28 John Paul II, *Letter to Women*, 2.
29 John Paul II, *Mulieris Dignitatem*, 18.

Wives, too, bring the gift of femininity to the family and through the family into the world. In the "economy of signs," they make present to the world something of the gift of the Bride, the Church, to the love of the divine Bridegroom. They irrevocably join their future to that of their husbands, in a relationship of mutual giving, at the service of love and life.[30]

Daughters and sisters bring the "feminine genius" to the heart of the family. They bring the richness of their sensitivity, their intuitiveness, their generosity and fidelity,[31] and in doing so, enrich the world.

Without detracting from the unique and foundational role of women in the family, the Holy Father urges us to "strive convincingly to ensure that the widest possible space is open to women in all areas of culture, economics, politics and ecclesial life itself, so that all human society is increasingly enriched by the gifts proper to masculinity and femininity."[32] For "without the contribution of women, society is less alive, culture impoverished, and peace less stable."[33] "Especially," he writes, "when the ultimate questions about life are at stake. Who is man? What is his destiny? What is the meaning of life?" he asks, "How could the feminine mind be undervalued? Women's entrance into the world of culture in all its branches—from philosophy to theology, from the social to the natural sciences, from the figurative arts to music—is a hopeful sign for humanity."[34] He confides in us that "the Church looks to women to do even more to save society from the deadly virus of degradation and violence which is today witnessing a dramatic increase."[35] In the words of Edith Stein, "The nation … doesn't simply need what we have. It needs who we are."[36]

In his letter to us, John Paul II renews the Church's commitment to welcoming the contribution of women, turning "to the *attitude of Jesus Christ himself*," who "transcend[ed] the established norms of his culture, treat[ing] women with openness, respect, acceptance and tenderness." In the sacrament of Baptism, the Lord bestows on us a share in the "prophetic, priestly and royal mission of Christ." We share in his "royal priesthood" by presenting our bodies as a living sacrifice, whole and acceptable to God (cf. Rom 12:1), by giving witness to Christ in every place, and by giving an explanation to anyone who asks the reason for the hope in eternal life that is in us (cf. 1 Pt 3:15).[37]

30 See John Paul II, *Letter to Women*, 2.
31 Ibid.
32 John Paul II, "The Feminine Genius," 1, in *The Genius of Women*, p. 27.
33 Ibid.
34 John Paul II, "Closing the Gap between the Cultural Opportunities for Men and Women," 2, in *The Genius of Women*, p. 31.
35 John Paul II, "Welcome to Gertrude Mongella," 5, in *The Genius of Women*, p. 41.
36 Edith Stein, "Women's Value in National Life," In *Essays on Woman*, trans. Freda Mary Oben (Washington, DC: ICS Publications, 1987).
37 See John Paul II, *Mulieris Dignitatem*, 27.

Christ invited women in a special way to participate in his prophetic mission as he walked the earth spreading the Good News of his kingdom, and they were primary witnesses of his Passion and Resurrection. In his 1995 *Holy Thursday Letter to Priests*, John Paul II highlighted women's participation in the prophetic mission of Christ and urged priests throughout the world to "guarantee the participation of everyone—men and women alike—in the threefold prophetic, priestly and royal mission of Christ."[38]

Our Holy Father draws our attention to a few of our older sisters in the faith who faithfully carried out the mission of sharing the "Good News" of Christ, including "the Samaritan woman and her dialogue with Christ at Jacob's well in Sychar (cf. Jn 4:1-42): It is to her, a Samaritan woman and a sinner, that Jesus reveals the depths of the true worship of God, who is concerned not about the place but rather about the attitude of worship 'in spirit and truth.'"[39] He also speaks of "the sisters of Lazarus, Mary and Martha." Mary, the more contemplative of the two, is honored in the Gospel of Luke, by Christ, who "gives preeminence to contemplation over activity … It is to her sister Mary, the more 'active' of the two, that Jesus reveals the profound mysteries of his mission; 'I am the resurrection and the life; he who believes in me, though he dies, yet shall he shall live, and whoever lives and believes in me shall never die.' (Jn 11:25-26)."[40] "The paschal mystery," the Holy Father writes, "is summed up in these words addressed to a woman."[41]

Speaking of the Passion narrative, John Paul II writes, "Is it not an incontestable fact that women were the ones closest to Christ along the way of the cross and at the hour of his death? A man, Simon of Cyrene, is forced to carry the cross (cf. Mt 27:32); but many women of Jerusalem spontaneously show him compassion along the ***via crucis*** (cf. Lk 23:27). The figure of Veronica, albeit not biblical, expresses well the feelings of the women of Jerusalem along the ***via dolorosa***."[42]

He continues, "Beneath the cross there is only one apostle, John, the son of Zebedee, whereas there are several women (cf. Mt 27:55-56): the mother of Christ … Salome, the mother of the sons of Zebedee, John and James; Mary, the mother of James the Less and Joseph; and Mary Magdalene. All these women were fearless witnesses to Jesus' agony; all were present at the anointing and the laying of his body in the tomb. After his burial, as the day before the Sabbath draws to a close, they depart, but with the intention

Via crucis is Latin for the "way of the Cross."

Via dolorosa is Latin for the "way of suffering."

NOTES

38 John Paul II, "Holy Thursday Letter to Priests," 7, in *The Genius of Women*, p. 71.
39 Ibid., p. 69.
40 Ibid.
41 Ibid.
42 Ibid.

of returning as soon as it is allowed. And it is they who will be the ones to tell the apostles (cf. Jn 20:1-2). Mary Magdalene, lingering at the tomb in tears, is the first to meet the Risen One, who sends her to the apostles as the first herald of his resurrection (cf. Jn 20:11-18). With good reason, therefore, the Easter tradition places Mary Magdalene on a par with the apostles, since she was the first to proclaim the truth of the resurrection, followed by the apostles and Christ's disciples."[43]

Just as he invited those early women to share in his prophetic mission two thousand years ago, he invites each one of us here and now, today, to "[g]o into all the world and preach the gospel to the whole creation."[44] "In the spirit of those great Christian women who have enlightened the life of the Church throughout the centuries and who have often called the Church back to her essential mission and service," John Paul II calls upon us: "I make an appeal to the women of the Church today *to assume new forms of leadership in service*, and I appeal to all the institutions of the Church to welcome this contribution."[45]

Into the heart of the family, the Church and the world, we are invited to be a "prophetic voice," "*reconciling people with life*" and bearing "*witness to the meaning of genuine love*."[46] Like a young man on bended knee, the Lord has proposed his love to us and invites us to share our lives with him. When we "see the person with our hearts," in "their greatness and limitations," when we "go out and help them,…the basic plan of the Creator takes flesh in the history of humanity and there is constantly revealed, in the variety of vocations, that *beauty*— not merely physical, but above all spiritual—which God bestowed from the very beginning on all, and in a particular way on women."[47] As we ponder our incredible and urgent mission, may we remember John Paul II's call to "Be not afraid! Open wide the doors to Christ!" to which Pope Benedict XVI adds, "For he gives you everything and takes nothing away."[48] May Mary, the highest expression of the "feminine genius," the "Queen of the Apostles," and the model for and prototype of the Church and every Christian, help us to imitate her *fiat* and teach us how make of our lives a generous gift to the One who loves us so much that he would rather die than live without us. John Paul II—John Paul the Great—pray for us.

43 Ibid., pp. 69-70.
44 Mark 16:15
45 John Paul II, "Letter to Mary Ann Glendon," in *The Genius of Women*, p. 62, emphasis mine.
46 John Paul II, *Evangelium Vitae*, 99.
47 John Paul II, *Letter to Women*, 12.
48 "Homily of His Holiness Benedict XVI," Mass, Imposition of the Pallium and Conferral of the Fisherman's Ring for the Beginning of the Petrine Ministry of the Bishop of Rome, St. Peter's Square, Sunday, 24 April 2005; available from www.vatican.va/holy_father/benedict_xvi/homilies/2005/documents/hf_ben-xvi_hom_20050424_inizio-pontificio-en.html; Internet, accessed 1 May 2005, recalling Pope John Paul II's proclamation at the beginning of his pontificate on 22 October 1978.

DISCUSSION QUESTIONS

1. Does the "feminine genius" limit us to specific spheres of influence, or is it a gift that we can bring anywhere?

2. Do you invest enough time in making human relations more authentic? Is the Holy Spirit calling you to give more of yourself—your time, your friendship, your prayers—to someone in your life?

3. Think of one way—big or small—that you can be a prophetic voice, calling the world back to a "priority of love" by making each of these areas more authentic:

   a. Your family

   b. Your workplace (if you work outside the home)

   c. The Church

   d. Your community

NOTES

4. John Paul II addressed the *Letter to Women* to each and every woman throughout the world. Are there women in your life who do not know that he has written to them, too? Think of the women that you know. How do you think his letter might touch their hearts?

5. How would the world be different than it is today if more women (and men) received his message and acted upon it?

6. The last step of the Examination of Conscience that we spoke about at the beginning of the study is to make a resolution. When our lives have been changed by Christ, we cannot sit idly by and let ourselves continue in paths of mediocrity. We have been called to excellence. What will be your first step, your first resolution, in utilizing what you have learned "at the service of humanity, of peace, of the spread of God's kingdom?"

For Personal Meditation

I make an appeal to the women of Church today to assume new forms of leadership in service, and I appeal to all the institutions of the Church to welcome this contribution.

—John Paul II

What Happened at Beijing

Mary Ann Glendon

"You are going to Beijing to be witnesses," the Holy See's Undersecretary for Relations with States told us as we left for the UN's Fourth World Conference on Women last September-daunting words for our band of fourteen women and eight men from nine countries and five continents. In the turmoil of the next two weeks, however, the idea of being witnesses helped our diverse group to coalesce into a unified team that would work, first, to make the documents issued by the conference more responsive to the actual lives of women, and, second-in keeping with the Catholic Church's traditional mission to the poor-to be a voice for the marginalized and voiceless women who can seldom make themselves heard in the corridors of power.

We hoped to avoid the situation that developed at the UN's 1994 Conference on Population and Development in Cairo, where an abortion rights initiative led by a hard-edged U.S. delegation pushed all other population and development issues into the background. The Holy See's efforts to correct that skewed emphasis never got through to the public. [See George Weigel, "What Happened at Cairo," FT, February 1995-Eds.] For the most part, the press accepted the population lobby's caricature of the Vatican at Cairo as anti-woman, anti-sex, and in favor of unrestrained procreation.

Before the Beijing conference opened, indications were that most nations had little disposition to reopen the fragile consensus that had been reached at Cairo. The idea that abortion was a legitimate tool of population control had been expressly rejected in the Cairo document. The U.S. administration, chastened by the November 1994 elections, was unlikely to openly lead another controversial charge. And in any event, the Beijing conference was not a population conference; its mandate was "Action for Equality, Development, and Peace." On those topics, we believed, the Holy See's positions, drawn from the Church's teachings on social and economic justice, stood a better chance of being heard. Our hopes in that regard were only slightly dimmed by our growing awareness that few media people had a clear idea of the subject and scope of the Beijing conference.

The failure of the press (and even many delegates) to do their homework was understandable. The Beijing documents (a brief Declaration and a long-winded Program of Action) were a 149-page (single-spaced) hodge- podge of the good, the bad, and the silly. To a lawyer's eye, they resembled a sprawling piece of legislation, with slabs of ideological pork interspersed among commonsense provisions and bureaucratic boilerplate. They had been produced, naturally, by a committee-the UN Commission on the Status of Women.

The drafting process, through two preparatory conferences, was heavily influenced by population control lobbyists and old-line, hard-line feminist groups. Negotiators from members of the UN and its specialized agencies reached agreement fairly easily on the bulk of the provisions, but a large proportion of the draft documents went to Beijing in brackets, signifying that no accord could be reached at the preparatory stage.

From the beginning, the documents were at war with themselves in several respects. Many provisions addressed issues of equal opportunity, education, and development in a sensible way. But reading the drafts overall, one would have no idea that most women marry, have children, and are urgently concerned with how to mesh family life with participation in broader social and economic spheres. The implicit vision of women's progress was based on the model-increasingly challenged by men and women alike-in which family responsibilities are avoided or subordinated to personal advancement. When dealing with health, education, and young girls, the drafts emphasized sex and reproduction to the neglect of many other crucial issues. The overall effect was like the leaning tower of Pisa, admirable from some angles, but unbalanced, and resting on a shaky foundation.

The first morning's colorful opening ceremony in the Great Hall of the People was an odd mixture of the sublime and the silly-as though replicating the conference documents. Mistresses of ceremonies who appeared to be on loan from the trade show commissariat presided in sequinned evening gowns over a program that mingled ballet dancers and hula-hula girls, a performance by the Chinese Women's Philharmonic orchestra and a parade of fashions, world-class gymnastics and a martial arts display where the women vanquished all the men.

That was the last hour of relaxation our delegation had until the conference ended. Our negotiators, four women and three men, worked virtually around the clock for the next two weeks in as many as seven separate, concurrent sessions, dealing with the knotty problems that had been left for resolution in Beijing. The rest of us tried to collect and read reams of conference documents, to maintain a presence of at least two persons in the plenary session, to staff our makeshift headquarters, and to "witness" in our communications with other delegations, the media, and Catholics attending the parallel women's forum in Huairou.

We were heartened by Pakistani Prime Minister Benazir Bhutto's speech in the opening plenary session. Mrs. Bhutto zeroed in on some of the defects in the documents. They were, she said, "disturbingly weak" on the role of the traditional family and on the connection between family disintegration and general moral decay. At a subsequent session, U.S. First Lady Hillary Rodham Clinton was clearly mindful of the Senate's bipartisan resolution instructing American delegates not to denigrate motherhood and the family. She condemned direct coercion in population control programs and made several positive references to women's roles as mothers and family members.

Mrs. Clinton's carefully worded speech was just one of many signs that the U.S. had drastically overhauled its strategy since Cairo. Throughout the Beijing conference, the American delegation avoided taking the initiative on controversial issues. They maintained an appearance of cordiality toward the Holy See, skirting open confrontation in negotiations. Members of the U.S. delegation frequently described the Vatican delegation to the press as "conciliatory"-as though we, not they, had changed since Cairo. Some of the beans were spilled by one American negotiator, after she had piped up briefly in favor of rights based on sexual orientation. Later, she told two members of the Holy See team she had momentarily forgotten that "we were told not to speak out on that one."

In my opening statement, I reaffirmed the positions the Holy See had taken at previous conferences, and called attention to several areas where the Beijing drafts needed to be improved. The documents barely mentioned marriage, motherhood, and the family-except negatively as impediments to women's self-realization (and as associated with violence and oppression). The women's health section focused disproportionately on sexual and reproductive matters, with scarcely a glance toward nutrition, sanitation, tropical diseases, access to basic health services, or even maternal morbidity and mortality. Women's poverty was addressed in narrow terms as chiefly a problem of equality between women and men, slighting the influence of family breakdown and unjust economic structures. I pointed out that, without recognition and support of their roles in child-raising, effective equality would remain elusive for far too many women. I concluded with the observation that there can be no real progress for women, or men, at the expense of children or of the underprivileged.

These points seemed so reasonable to us that, in the first few days of the conference, we were confident that they would find wide support. Ominous signs, however, soon appeared. Some delegations from developing countries seemed less independent than at Cairo. Holy See negotiators were often receiving short shrift from chairpersons wielding heavy gavels. The procedural difficulties became acute in sessions dealing with the controversial health sections of the draft. Many otherwise inactive delegations showed up, and the negotiating room became especially crowded and chaotic. At one point, when our negotiator attempted to intervene in support of a bracketed paragraph urging that women be informed of the health risks of promiscuity and certain contraceptive methods, the Chair ruled her out of order on grounds that the Holy See, as a Permanent Observer, did not even have the right to vote. By the time the Chair was forced to retract that mistake, the language in question had been eliminated. The tenor of discussion on the issue is captured by the remark of an Egyptian delegate: "If we start telling women about the harmful effects of contraceptives, they might not use them anymore."

By Thursday of the first week, our negotiators were bringing back news of another unexpected development. A minority coalition, led by the powerful fifteen-member European Union negotiating as a bloc, was pushing a version of the sexual and abortion rights agenda that had been rejected by the Cairo conference. The EU-led coalition was so intent on its unfinished Cairo agenda that it was stalling negotiations on other issues. Equally disturbing, the coalition was taking positions with ominous implications for universal human rights.

Joined by a few other countries (Barbados, Canada, Namibia, South Africa), the EU was opposing the inclusion of key, pertinent principles from UN instruments where the nations of the world had recognized certain core rights and obligations as universal. The controversy centered on five crucial areas:

1. To bring the treatment of marriage and the family more into line with women's actual needs and aspirations, the Holy See and other negotiators had proposed references to standard international language. The UN Universal Declaration of Human Rights was an obvious source. It makes marriage a fundamental right, and provides that "the family is the natural and fundamental group unit of society and is entitled to protection by society and the state" (Art. 16). The EU coalition not only opposed that language, but pressed to pluralize "family" wherever it appeared in the documents. This move would have been innocent enough if it simply referred to the fact that there is no single form of family organization. But here it seemed intended to place a range of alternative

life styles on the same legal footing as families founded on kinship or marriage, undermining the legal preferences that many countries accord to child-raising families.

2. Similarly, the coalition contested every effort to include the word "motherhood" except where it appeared in a negative light, even though the Universal Declaration provides that "Motherhood and childhood are entitled to special care and assistance" (Art. 25).

3. The coalition sought to remove all references to religion, morals, ethics, or spirituality, except where religion was portrayed as associated with intolerance or extremism. During one stormy negotiating session on women's health, an EU negotiator even opposed a reference to codes of medical ethics, insisting, astonishingly, that "ethics have no place in medicine." The coalition also objected to a paragraph providing for freedom of conscience and religion in the context of education, in spite of the Universal Declaration's provision that "Everyone has the right to freedom of thought, conscience, and religion . . . [including] freedom, either alone or in community with others and in public or private, to manifest his religion or belief in teaching, practice, worship, and observance" (Art. 18).

4. Though the Beijing documents had identified the situation of the "girl child" as a "critical area," the coalition attempted to eliminate all recognition of parental rights and duties from the draft, even rejecting direct quotations from the Convention on the Rights of the Child. They seemed indifferent to the fact that the Universal Declaration and subsequent human rights documents have consistently protected the parent-child relationship from outside intrusion.

5. Finally, the coalition made strenuous efforts to remove references to "human dignity" as used in the Preamble of the Universal Declaration of Human Rights: "Recognition of inherent human dignity and of the equal and inalienable rights of all members of the human family" is the very "foundation of freedom, justice, and peace." They apparently feared that dignity language might legitimate departures from the equality principle. Equality and dignity, however, are inseparable in the Declaration. To eliminate dignity is to undermine the concept that human rights, including equality, belong to all men and women by virtue of their inherent worth as human beings, rather than existing at the whim of this or that political regime.

The EU caucus' assault on key provisions of the universal human rights corpus was something of a mystery. Europe, after all, prides itself on being the cradle and custodian of many of these ideas. More puzzling still, the EU negotiators' stances on these matters were at variance with similar provisions in most of their own national constitutions and with the underlying principles of their own family assistance programs.

In the stark vision promoted by the EU caucus at Beijing, there is no room for the idea that society has a special interest in providing the best possible conditions for raising children. Family life, marriage, and motherhood would be worthy of no more protection than any other ways in which adults choose to order their lives. The girl child, her parents nowhere visible, would be alone with her rights. A document embodying that vision would cast a shadow over programs and policies that provide assistance to child-raising families, just at a time when most countries are already curtailing their social expenditures. A document on women's issues from which all positive references to motherhood and family life were removed would send a discouraging message to women who take pride and satisfaction in family roles.

The EU negotiators' positions can be explained in part by a phenomenon Americans know well-the tendency when arguing for a favorite right to brush aside all other rights and obligations. The EU-led coalition was so single-minded in its determination to seed the Beijing documents with sexual and reproductive rights that it was willing to let important competing values go by the boards. At least that was how it seemed when the Holy See's Ambassador to the UN, Archbishop Renato Martino, and I met with Christina Alberdi, leader of the European Union caucus, and, later on the same day, with several members of the French delegation. We raised our concerns about human rights issues at both meetings. The delegates and their assistants listened politely, thanked us for our point of view, but were not forthcoming with any explanation.

After several similar encounters, I was reminded of the Cook County criminal courts of the 1960s, when occasionally the rumor would go around the corridors that "the fix was in" on a particular case. I began to wonder whether a blend of sexism and political expediency had induced some governments to regard the women's conference as unimportant in itself, and thus to treat delegation appointments as handy sops to throw to old-line feminists and population control zealots. That would explain the now unmistakable emergence of an unfinished Cairo agenda, the hot pursuit of sexual rights, and the efforts to make sure that parents would not come between their daughters and those who know better than her parents.

While our negotiators struggled to break that impasse, others of us spent many hours talking with representatives of various Catholic organizations who had been attending the women's forum at Huairou. We listened carefully to the different points of view they brought to the documents. One particularly impressive group was the Neo-Catechumens- intelligent, dedicated, lay missionaries who work among the neediest populations in the poorest parts of the world. They had followed the conference closely, and, at the end of the first week, urged the Holy See to reject the documents in their entirety. The Declaration and Program of Action were, in their view, so permeated with a false anthropology, so obsessed with sexuality to the exclusion of other issues, so profoundly subversive of the good for women, that the best way for the Church to witness to the truth would be to denounce them and decline to join the Conference consensus. As matters stood then, that was a live option.

Later that day, several members of our delegation made ourselves available for general discussion with Catholic groups. A glance around the crowded meeting room, however, revealed that the gathering had also drawn several inquisitive journalists, the doyenne of American feminism Betty Friedan, and members of the anti-Catholic, population control front group that calls itself Catholics for a Free Choice. Few comments from this assembly directly concerned conference issues. The chief preoccupations of most who spoke seemed to be power, sex, and the Catholic Church herself.

A great many critical remarks on decision-making power within the Church and the male priesthood came from Catholic women who seemed depressingly unfamiliar with basic principles of religious freedom, with the dynamic feminism of John Paul II, or with the vast range of opportunities for female and lay participation in Church activities, processes, and ministries. Even some women with religious vocations seemed to think of the priesthood as a powerful "job" that ought to be made available on an equal opportunity basis, rather than a calling to humble self- sacrificing service.

Many of those with whom we met seemed not to realize the number of opportunities for important service going begging because there are not enough women or men with the time, desire, and dedication to help. I urged them to respond to John Paul II's call for women to "assume new forms of leadership in service," noting his simultaneous call to the institutions of the Church "to welcome this contribution of women."

Meanwhile, we had reached conference midpoint, and negotiations were still stalled. It seemed unlikely that the EU caucus' negotiating stances reflected government policy or public opinion in their home countries. On Friday night, we composed a press release calling attention to the conflicts between the positions being taken at Beijing by the EU caucus and settled principles of national and international law.

By Monday, there was a marked change in the negotiating atmosphere. Questions had begun to be posed in European legislatures, including the EU Parliament, concerning what their delegations were up to in faraway Beijing. "Why did you have to bring all this out in the open?" complained one EU delegate who was apparently unfamiliar with the concept of government in the sunshine. Negotiations began moving swiftly, and the text began to change in some key respects. The final documents were rapidly taking shape, section by section, in different negotiating rooms, and seemed to be moving toward something we might be able to accept-at least in part.

The picture in the end was mixed. Many of the best provisions-on women's education, poverty, the environment, and peace-are likely to wither unless supported by major financial commitments and nurtured by well- thought-out programs, while other provisions actually threaten both universal human rights and the well-being of women.

In favor of the Holy See's associating itself with the documents to some extent, nevertheless, there were a number of considerations. The heart of the Program for Action consists of many provisions that are consonant with Catholic teachings on dignity, freedom, and social justice: those dealing with the needs of women in poverty; with strategies for development, literacy, and education; for ending violence against women; for building a culture of peace; and with providing access for women to employment, land, capital, and technology. Other worthwhile provisions concerned the connection between the feminization of poverty and family disintegration, the relation of environmental degradation to scandalous patterns of production and consumption, the discrimination against women that begins with abortion of female fetuses, the promotion of partnership and mutual respect between men and women, and the need for reform of the international economic order. The specific economic recommendations mark a healthy break from the discredited Marxist ideas that once prevailed at UN gatherings. Many central ideas, moreover, had been introduced by or with the help of the Holy See over the years (e.g., the emphasis on women's education, and the insistence that the human being must be at the center of concern in development).

Even the worst parts of the draft documents had undergone some improvement, thanks to the efforts of our tireless and talented negotiators, Msgr. Frank Dewane, Patricia Donahoe, John Klink, Msgr. Diarmuid Martin, Janne Matlary, Gail Quinn, and Sheri Rickert. In the preparatory conferences, they had introduced equal educational opportunity for refugees; "general access" for women, as well as "equal access," to education; and the reference to women's roles as peace educators in the family and society. By the end of the conference, they had secured references to relevant universal rights and obligations in all five areas where those concepts had been threatened.

A few swallows, admittedly, do not make a summer. The positive changes tempered the tone of the documents and maintained continuity with the rights tradition that will inform future interpretations. But the documents are still seriously unbalanced. The Cairo principle that abortion must not be promoted as a method of family planning was eventually reaffirmed, but the Cairo language on support for parental rights and responsibilities and respect for religious and cultural values is stronger than in parallel provisions in the Beijing documents.

Though EU efforts to gain inclusion of the phrase "sexual rights" were rebuffed, the final documents do contain ambiguous rights language in the areas of sexuality and fertility. A paragraph in the health section, for example, speaks of women's "right to have control over and decide freely and responsibly on matters related to their sexuality, including sexual and reproductive health, free of coercion, discrimination, and violence." The U.S. was well-satisfied with this result, according to a post-conference memorandum from Undersecretary of State for Global Affairs Timothy Wirth to members of the American delegation. Wirth's evaluation of the Beijing Platform was that it "met the U.S. government's goals (reaffirm important commitments made at previous international conferences, including human rights of women in reproductive health and rights)."

There was no consensus on what the vague new language means beyond the rights to say no and be free of sexual exploitation. By general agreement, it does not cover sexual orientation, Canada's energetic efforts to introduce rights in that area having encountered broad opposition at the conference.

Arguments will no doubt be made that references to women's rights "to control all aspects of their health, in particular their own fertility" implicitly recognize abortion as a human right. Such an interpretation is excluded, however, by Paragraph 107(k), a direct quotation from Cairo, which provides: "Any measures or changes related to abortion within the health system can only be determined at the national or local level according to the national legislative process." This language was necessary in view of the fact that, unlike the United States and China, most countries restrict and strictly regulate abortion. Even nations like Sweden with relatively permissive abortion laws do not follow the U.S. in characterizing abortion as a "right." Paragraph 107(k) contains other language that militates against abortion as a fundamental right: "reduce recourse to abortion," "eliminate the need for abortion," "help avoid repeat abortion." One would hardly say of an important right like free speech, for example, that governments should reduce it, eliminate the need for it, and help avoid its repetition.

Even if there were no such specific language in the Cairo and Beijing documents, it is a basic principle of interpretation that fundamental rights cannot be created or destroyed by implication. Moreover, the Beijing conference had no authority to add to or tinker with the corpus of universal human rights. The UN historically has conducted that process with great care and gravity, most recently at the 1993 Human Rights Conference in Vienna. It would indeed be a dark day if human rights could be revised in disorderly negotiating sessions such as those where the Beijing health sections were rammed through.

As at Cairo, the Holy See was concerned that language on sexual and reproductive "health" would be used to promote the quick-fix approach to getting rid of poverty by getting rid of poor people. Much of the foundation money that swirled around the Beijing process was aimed at forging a link between development aid and programs that pressure poor women into abortion, sterilization, and use of risky contraceptive methods. That point has also troubled distinguished non-Catholic observers. In the wake of Cairo, Harvard economist-philosopher Amartya Sen criticized a "dangerous tendency" on the part of developed nations to search for solutions to overpopulation that "treat the people involved not as reasonable beings, allies faced with a common problem, but as impulsive and uncontrolled sources of great social harm, in need of strong discipline." Sen charged that by giving priority to "family planning arrangements in the Third World countries over other commitments such as education and health care," international policy makers "produce negative effects on people's well-being and reduce their freedoms." In a similar vein, the British medical journal Lancet blasted the Beijing documents for a "new colonialism" designed to control rather than liberate women.

The Holy See's position as the conference came to an end was thus a difficult one. The documents had been improved in some respects. But in other ways they were even more disappointing than the Cairo document, which the Holy See had been able to join only partially and with many formal reservations. After an intense session in which members of our delegation shared their views, hopes, doubts, and concerns about the documents, our assessment of their pros and cons was communicated to the Vatican Secretariat of State. On Thursday morning, we received the Holy Father's decision: accept what is positive, but vigorously reject what cannot be accepted.

Accordingly, the Holy See delegation associated itself in part, with several reservations, with the conference documents. As at Cairo, it reaffirmed its well-known positions on abortion and family planning methods. It could not accept the health section at all. A controversy over the word "gender" that loomed before the conference had been largely defused with a consensus that gender was to be understood according to ordinary usage in the United Nations context. The Holy See, however, deemed it prudent to attach to its reservations a further, more nuanced, statement of interpretation, in which it dissociated itself from rigid biological determinism as well as from the notion that sexual identity is indefinitely malleable. In keeping with the Holy Father's instruction to vigorously reject what was unacceptable, my concluding statement on behalf of the Holy See was sharply critical of the conference documents for the remaining deficiencies that our delegation had tried from the beginning to publicize and remedy.

The most important political lesson to be taken from the Beijing conference is that huge international conferences are not suitable settings for addressing complex questions of social and economic justice or grave issues of human rights. Unfortunately, there is an increasing tendency for advocates of causes that have failed to win acceptance through ordinary dem-ocratic processes to resort to the international arena, far removed (they hope) from scrutiny and accountability. The sexual libertarians, old-line feminists, and coercive population controllers can be expected to keep on trying to insert their least popular ideas into UN documents for unveiling at home as "international norms."

A number of lingering questions about Beijing merit the attention of investigative reporters. What deals did the affluent nations make with their client states? Why did the EU caucus champion an agenda so far removed from the urgent concerns of most of the world's women? Why did delegates from countries with strong family protection provisions in their constitutions (e.g., Germany, Ireland, Italy) not break ranks with the EU when it attacked the spirit of those provisions? Why were the conference documents so skewed from the beginning? Who paid for the voyages of thousands of lobbyists at Huairou whose main interest was not in women's needs and rights, but in controlling women's fertility?

American delegate Geraldine Ferraro's description of the Beijing conference as marking an end to the North-South conflicts that have plagued UN conferences in the past was disingenuous. The delegations from affluent countries that battled so boldly at Cairo or Beijing for their ideas about population control and sexual rights were timid as mice when it came to making commitments of resources. In defiance of evidence that economic development and women's education lead to lowered fertility rates, the developed countries made it clear they wanted population control on the cheap. The relative silence of Third World delegates on issues vital to women in their own countries was bewildering. How can one explain that many delegations from poor nations came to sessions involving sexual and reproductive matters with well- prepared position papers, yet were absent or silent when resources and other crucial issues were discussed? Since many of those same delegations entered formal reservations at the end of the conference, chances are the folks back home will never suspect that their representatives did not speak up in negotiations where a few strong voices could have made a difference.

The significance of the Beijing documents should neither be exaggerated nor minimized. The Declaration and Platform are nonbinding documents that may or may not serve as international guidelines for the way various private and public actors deal with the issues they cover. The authority of the worst parts of the documents is diminished by their vagueness, their inconsistency with respected international documents, and by the unusually large number of UN members who expressed dissent. When 43 of 181 nations present have formally registered serious concerns, it is hard to speak of a consensus. The authority of the constructive sections, on the other hand, is supported by consensus and amplified by their similarity to provisions in documents from other international conferences, most recently the Copenhagen Summit on Social Development.

The significance of Beijing for human rights is mainly in the nature of a warning. As the fiftieth anniversary of the UN's 1948 Universal Declaration of Human Rights approaches, the Beijing conference appears to have been a testing ground for certain ideas and approaches that will be advanced again. We have not seen the last of the effort to make abortion a fundamental right, or of the attempt to depose heterosexual marriage and child-raising families from their traditionally preferred positions. Neither have we seen the last of selective use of rights language to advance an anti-rights agenda-exemplified at Beijing by the emphasis on formal equality at the expense of motherhood's special claim to protection, and by the elimination of most references to religion and parental rights. Worrisome, too, is the trivialization of universally recognized core principles through the attempted addition of vague new rights.

All this is familiar stuff to Americans. At the international level, it is evidence of the continuing colonization of the universal language of human rights by an impoverished dialect that has already made great inroads on political discourse in the United States. Its features include: rights envisioned without corresponding individual or social responsibilities; one's favorite rights touted as absolute with others ignored; the rights-bearer imagined as radically autonomous and self- sufficient; and the willy-nilly proliferation of new rights.

That dialect contrasts with the broad, rich, and balanced Universal Declaration where the individual rights-bearer's dignity is resoundingly affirmed, but the family is recognized as the basic social unit. In the Universal Declaration, fundamental individual rights are simultaneously affirmed and situated within the social contexts that determine whether rights, freedom, and dignity will become realities: "In the exercise of his rights and freedoms, everyone shall be subject only to such limitations as are determined by law solely for the purpose of securing due recognition and respect for the rights and freedoms of others and of meeting the just requirements of morality, public order, and the general welfare in a democratic society."

Not least alarming about the assault on the human rights tradition by powerful actors at Beijing is that it went virtually unreported. As far as the American press was concerned, the human rights story was the Chinese treatment of Harry Wu. To European journalists, it was the failed efforts of a few Islamic countries to authorize opting out of certain equality measures on cultural and religious grounds. The U.S. was correct, of course, to condemn brazen violations of universal rights. The Europeans were right, too, that human rights ought not to be nullified by cultural exceptions. But neither should the catalog of human rights be redefined and expanded to "universalize" the highly individualistic ideologies of modernizing elites. Nor must human rights be sharply separated from the cultural and religious contexts in which rights are rooted and protected. Nor must the corpus of core rights and obligations be casually altered. As memories fade about why it was necessary after World War II to affirm the existence of certain inalienable rights, the citizens of the world must be vigilant to prevent trivialization and dilution of those basic protections of human dignity.

In the end, one may hope that the good in the nonbinding Beijing documents will survive and flourish-especially since, as any good feminist would say, they must be seen in context. The context in this case is the framework of the overarching universal human rights tradition.

John Paul II's instruction to his Beijing delegation reflected the approach he has taken to women's issues in his writings. In the 1995 *World Day of Peace* message, he noted that "when one looks at the great process of women's liberation," one sees that the journey has been a difficult one, with its "share of mistakes," but headed toward a better future for women and the entire human family. In his recent *Letter to Women*, he added, "This journey must go on!" It is characteristic of this Pope that, in confronting flawed human enterprises of various sorts, he seeks to find and build on what is sound and healthy, while identifying and criticizing what is likely to be harmful to human flourishing.

Looking toward the future, the Pope stressed in his pre-conference message to Secretary-General Gertrude Mongella that the success of the gathering will depend on whether it offers a "vision capable of sustaining objective and realistic responses to the struggle and frustration that continue to be a part of all too many women's lives." Ultimately, it is up to concerned citizens, women and men, to bring the seedlings of "equality, development, and peace" to full flower, and to protect them from the encroaching culture of death. Fortunately, we do not garden alone. Not only are we surrounded by a cloud of witnesses, but divine grace is always operating in the world, inviting us to cooperate with it in building the civilization of life and love.

Mary Ann Glendon, who led the Vatican delegation to the Beijing Conference, is the Learned Hand Professor of Law at Harvard University.

Cairo Conference
Background Summary

The political and ideological maneuverings at the International Conferences on Population and Development prior to the Beijing Conference on Women set the stage for the Beijing Conference.

The Cairo Conference was the third in a series of international population conferences. The first was convened in 1974 in Budapest, Hungary and the second was held in Mexico City, Mexico in 1984. In his article "What Really Happened at Cairo," papal biographer George Weigel explains that the most powerful planners of these committees generally held the belief that people were "essentially a problem, even a pollutant, rather than a resource; that social, political, economic and ecological catastrophe was right around the corner unless drastic steps were taken to stabilize and then reverse the world population trends."[1] But coercive government programs did not appeal to the supposed beneficiaries of "population control": namely, the countries of the developing world. Third World countries pleaded for their protection, retorting that development, not population reduction programs imposed by wealthy nations, would improve their situation.[2]

At the 1984 Mexico City conference, population control proponents who were looking for a "quick fix" to the problems of the Third World through extensive population reduction campaigns were flatly defeated. They came to Mexico City expecting the conference to give its approval to abortion on demand in the name of family-planning. Instead, attention was directed toward the brutal Chinese policy of coercive abortion. China established its one-child policy in 1979 in order to limit communist China's population growth. The rule limits couples to one child. Fines, pressures to abort a pregnancy, and even forced sterilization accompanied second or subsequent pregnancies. The fact that some population control advocates were willing to overlook the Chinese policy of coercive abortion demonstrated the lengths to which they were willing to go to obtain their objective. The Developing World, however, was not willing to follow suit. In the end, the conference, with support from the United States under the Reagan Administration, adopted a final report that clearly affirmed that abortion was not a legitimate means of population control.[3] This struck a sore spot for those at the UN and the World Bank, as well as the major activist NGOs like Planned Parenthood of America and the International Planned Parenthood Federation, who were intent on inflicting the Third World with population reduction programs.

When the 1992 American presidential election victory went to Bill Clinton, it opened wide the horizons for abortion rights activists. With an uncompromising commitment to abortion on demand at home and extensive "population control" abroad, the Clinton Administration's chief foreign aid administrator, J. Brian Atwood, announced a five-year, $75 million pledge to fund the activities of the International Planned Parenthood Federation "on the bizarre grounds that the 'core' of the chaos in Somalia, in which U.S. troops were then embroiled, was overpopulation. Somali vital statistics may not be the world's

1 George Weigel, "What Really Happened at Cairo," in *First Things* 50 (February 1995): p. 24. For a more information on the Cairo Conference and John Paul II's reactions to it, see Weigel, *Witness to Hope: the Biography of Pope John Paul II* (New York: HarperCollins Publishers, Inc., 2001), pp. 715-727.
2 Weigel, "What Really Happened at Cairo," pp. 24-25.
3 Ibid., p. 25. Respectable demographers maintain that there is no such thing as "overpopulation." Furthermore, what exactly constitutes "overpopulation" has never even been scientifically defined. These scholars argue that what we tend to think of the symptoms of "overpopulation"—disease, hunger, overcrowding, high infant mortality—are more accurately described as the consequences of poverty and material deprivation. On this point, see Amartya Sen, "Population: Delusion and Reality," and Nicholas Eberstadt, "The Premises of Population Policy: A Reexamination," in *The Nine Lives of Population Control*, ed. Michael Cromartie (Grand Rapids: Eerdmans, 1995).
It is worth pointing out that within three years of the Cairo conference, the UN's own demographic projections were forecasting zero world population growth by 2040 and depopulation thereafter. See Nicholas Eberstadt, "World Population Implosion?" *The Public Interest*, 129 (Fall 1997), pp. 3-22.

finest, but a reasonable estimate is that Somalia, whose territory is a little larger than that of California, Washington state, Maryland, and Massachusetts combined, had a population in 1992 of some seven million, forty million fewer than the aggregate population of those four states."[4]

The U.S. agenda at the UN was radically different under the Clinton Administration than it was under the Reagan Administration. Representatives of the International Planned Parenthood Federation played the roles of national representatives at official conferences. For example, the chairman of the preparatory committee for the 1994 Cairo Conference (Prep-Com III), Dr. Fred Sai, was usually introduced as the "representative of Ghana," but also happened to be the President of the International Planned Parenthood Federation. Not surprisingly, Prep-Com III resulted in a major increase in funding for imposed population control programs (from $6 billion to $17 billion by 2000), paid for by the American, Japanese and Scandinavian contributions to the UN Fund for Population Activities [UNFPA] and cutbacks in other UN programs for education, healthcare, industrial development and disaster relief.[5]

The Cairo draft document proposed establishing a new category of human rights: "reproductive rights." Shortly before Prep-Com III, on March 16, 1994, Secretary of State Warren Christopher sent a cable to all U.S. diplomatic stations abroad with the message "the U.S. believes that access to safe, legal, and voluntary abortion is a fundamental right to all women."[6] The document produced by the committee encouraged governments to "use the entertainment media, including radio and television soap operas and drama, folk theater, and other traditional media" to penetrate the culture so as to subtly change the way people think about the objectives of the well-to-do North in the poor, developing South.[7]

More than sixty representatives of International Planned Parenthood Federation went to Cairo as official national delegates from a variety of countries.[8] But the Cairo Conference was not as successful as was predicted. Weigel proposes several reasons why: nervousness from Latin America, resistance from Islamic nations, resentment of African countries of what they saw as Western cultural imperialism, and the moral power of John Paul II.[9] In the summer of 1994, the Pope gave a series of reflections at his public audiences preceding the Cairo Conference. Weigel accounts:

> In these reflections, the Pope emphasized that the right to life is a basic human right, 'written in human nature,' and the foundation of any meaningful scheme of 'human rights'; spoke of the family as the 'primary cell' of society and as a 'natural institution' with rights that any just state must respect; defined marriage 'as a stable union of a man and a woman who are committed to the reciprocal gift of self and open to creating new life, [which] is not only a Christian value, but an original value of creation'; defended the equal human dignity of women, insisted that women must not be reduced to being objects of male pleasure, and argued that 'perfection for woman is not to be like man, making herself masculine to the point of losing her specific qualities as a woman'; noting that sexuality has a 'language of its own service of love and cannot be lived at the purely instinctual level'; argued that stable marriages were essential for the welfare of children; pointed out that the Church does not support an 'ideology of fertility at all costs,' but rather proposes a marital ethic in which the decision 'whether or not to have a child' is not 'motivated by selfishness or carelessness, but by a prudent, conscious generosity that weighs the possibilities and circumstances, and especially gives priority to the welfare of the unborn child'; rejected

4   Ibid., pp. 25-26. See Dennis Proust, "Hostile U.N. Prep Session," *Catholic New York*, April 21, 1994. See also George Weigel's reconstruction of Prep-Com III, based on his post-conference interviews with two members
     of the Holy See delegation, Monsignor Diarmuid Martin and Ms. Gail Quinn, in Weigel, *Witness to Hope*, p. 719.
5   Weigel, "What Really Happened at Cairo," p. 26.
6   Ibid., p. 27.
7   Ibid., p. 26.
8   Ibid., p. 27.
9   Ibid., p. 28.

coercive or 'authoritarian' family planning programs as a violation of the married couple's basic human rights and argued that the foundations of justice in a state are undermined when it does not recognize the unborn child's moral claim to protection; declared that discrimination against women in 'the workplace, culture and politics' must be eliminated in the name of an 'authentic emancipation' that does not 'deprive woman herself of what is primarily or exclusively hers' and argued that radical individualism is inhuman, as is a 'sexuality apart from ethical references.'[10]

By the end of the summer, Vice President Al Gore, speaking for the U.S. delegation at the National Press Club in Washington on August 25th, said that "the US has not sought, does not seek, and will not seek an international right to abortion."[11] Yet this tune was dissonant with the one sung by the draft document, whose definition of "reproductive healthcare" included "pregnancy termination" thanks to a U.S. initiative.[12]

At the Cairo Conference, the U.S. delegation led the crusade for abortion and eugenic population control programs, pushing all other population and development issues to the background. Mary Ann Glendon, professor of law at Harvard University and the leader of the Holy See's delegation for the Beijing Conference, expressed her concern that "the Holy See's efforts to correct that skewed emphasis never got through to the public. For the most part, the press accepted the population lobby's caricature of the Vatican at Cairo as anti-woman, anti-sex, and in favor of unrestrained procreation."[13]

10 Ibid.
11 "Remarks Prepared for Delivery by Vice President Al Gore, National Press Club, Washington, D.C., Thursday, August 25, 1994" (Washington, D.C.: Office of the Vice President), p. 8.
12 In an unprecedented rebuke to a public official by the Vatican, John Paul II's spokesperson, Joaquin Navarro-Valls, pointed out that "The draft document, which has the United States as its principal sponsor, contradicts, in reality, Mr. Gore's statement." Quoted in Christine Gorman, "Clash of Wills in Cairo," *Time*, September 12, 1994, p. 56.
13 Glendon, "What Happened at Beijing," p. 30.

What Really Happened at Cairo

George Weigel

© 1995 *First Things* 50 (February 1995): 24-31. Reprinted by permission.

Gargantuan international conferences replete with diplomats, "international civil servants," various "nongovernmental organization" (NGO) representatives, and the world press have been a staple feature of world politics since the Second World War. One does not fear sinning against charity by suggesting that many of these extravaganzas (in which the international ruling class cavorts, off-hours, in the sybaritic style to which it has become accustomed) are, in the Bard's familiar words, "a tale told by an idiot, full of sound and fury, signifying nothing." But there are exceptions, and they can be important.

The Helsinki Conference on Security and Cooperation in Europe, which produced the "Helsinki Accords" in 1975, was one such exception. When Leonid Brezhnev signed the Helsinki Final Act in 1975, he probably thought he was taking out a ninety-nine-year lease on Stalin's external empire. As things turned out, he was signing its death warrant. For "Basket Three" of the Final Act pledged the signatory nations of Europe and North America to certain human rights commitments. And those commitments in turn inspired the formation of "Helsinki monitoring groups," which were to become the backbone of the human rights resistance in Central and Eastern Europe in the late 1970s and throughout the 1980s: groups that were essential to the nonviolent collapse of communism in the Revolution of 1989 and the New Russian Revolution of 1991.

The September 1994 International Conference on Population and Development in Cairo might be another such exception, with yet another ironic outcome. The UN bureaucrats, Scandinavian politicos, Clinton Administration "global affairs" mavens, radical environmentalists, feminists, and population controllers who planned the conference intended it to be nothing less than the Great Cairo Turkey Shoot: a political slaughter in which the enemies of "individual autonomy," "sustainable growth," "global carrying capacity," "reproductive rights," "gender equity," abortion-on-demand, and the sexual revolution would be utterly, decisively routed. But they were not. Indeed, the Cairo conference just may have marked a turning point in the international debate over population and development. It is too early to know for sure, but it is just possible that the radicals' attempt to take the Cairo conference by storm set in motion moral and cultural dynamics that will, over time, result in the defeat of the radicals' agenda.

Which, if it were to come to pass, would be a bouleversement of world-historical proportions.

II

Cairo was the third in a series of decennial international population conferences. The first International Conference on Population was held in 1974 at Budapest, and the second (under the enlarged banner of "Population and Development") was convened in Mexico City in 1984. Planning for both of these meetings, within the UN bureaucracy and among the thousands of NGO activists who participate in UN-sponsored programs, was dominated by strident doomsayers and hard-core population controllers of the Garrett Hardin/Paul Ehrlich ("the battle to feed all humanity is over") school. That people were essentially a problem, even a pollutant, rather than a resource; that social, political, economic, and ecological catastrophe was right around the corner, unless drastic steps were taken to stabilize and then reverse world population trends- these were the themes, familiar to even the most casual student of the American anti-natalist lobby, that set the agenda for Budapest and Mexico City.

As it happened, these notions, and the prescriptions for coercive, governmentally enforced programs of fertility reduction that flowed from them, did not sit well with many of the putative beneficiaries of "population control": namely, the countries of the developing world. At Budapest, for example, the population technocrats were challenged both empirically and culturally: empirically, in that it was made plain that population patterns varied widely around the world, as the result of a complex interaction of economic, social, and cultural factors; and culturally, in that it became clear that there were many different understandings of how population issues should be addressed, even among those who shared the belief that there was a "population problem." "Development is the best contraceptive" became the slogan (crude, but not inaccurate) that the Third World counterposed to the Hardin/Ehrlich anti-natalist hysteria of the well-to-do "North."

Ten years later, the population controllers suffered an outright defeat at Mexico City. Not satisfied with the results of their massive efforts to export mechanical and chemical means of contraception to the Third World (some of which had met considerable resistance on both moral- cultural and medical grounds), UN and private sector population agencies had increasingly turned to abortion as a means of family planning and population control. The Chinese policy of coercive abortion was, of course, the most draconian of such enterprises, but its extremism was merely the cruelest face of a general policy actively supported by the anti-natalists throughout the developing world. The population controllers came to Mexico City expecting the conference to give its sanction to abortion-on-demand, in the name of family planning. Yet they were soundly rebuffed. For the conference, with vigorous support from the Reagan Administration, adopted a final report that stated flatly that abortion was not a legitimate means of population control.

This was an ideological defeat for the population controllers, not least because the attention focused on the brutality of the Chinese program graphically demonstrated the lengths to which the controllers were willing to go; having seen what lay at the end of the road, some countries were prepared to question the legitimacy of embarking on the journey in the first place. But the Mexico City conference also had serious financial consequences: it resulted in restrictions on funding for abortion in UN programs; it eliminated such funding from the population components of many nations' foreign aid budgets; and, on the domestic front, it became the international legal instrument with which the Reagan and Bush Administrations forbade federal support for any public or private aid program that included abortion among its family planning activities.

As may be imagined, all of this stuck, hard, in the collective craw of the population controllers at the UN and World Bank, and among such major activist NGOs as Planned Parenthood of America and the International Planned Parenthood Federation. For not only had they suffered an ideological and financial defeat at Mexico City; they also seemed to understand, however dimly, that they had suffered a moral drubbing as well. It seemed that many people-by their lights unenlightened, authoritarian, conservative, to be sure, but influential nonetheless-believed that the population controllers were not only wrong, they were bad. And since a powerful conviction of its inherent righteousness has been perhaps the chief psychological characteristic of the population control movement for well over a century, it was this moral rejection that cut most deeply, and inflamed the controllers' determination to "go beyond Mexico City" at the next decennial conference.

The U.S. presidential election of November 1992 promised the population controllers relief, and indeed more than relief. Bill Clinton and Al Gore had, after all, run on the most radical "social issues" platform in American history, committing themselves to federal funding of abortion- on-demand in the U.S. at any stage of a pregnancy; deploring "explosive population growth" in the Third World; and pledging to use federal tax dollars to fund "greater family planning efforts" in U.S. foreign aid programs. Moreover, the Democratic Party's most vocal activists included men and women, heterosexual and homosexual, who were deeply committed to securing, in American law and public policy, the sexual revolution's core principle of individual autonomy and its severance of sexual relations from marriage. Little wonder, then, that the controllers, determined as they were to "go beyond Mexico City," read the electoral entrails of November 3, 1992 as a mandate for radical change in U.S. population policy and, a posteriori, in the agenda of the third International Conference on Population and Development, which was to be held in Cairo in September 1994.

Their expectations were met in full. Indeed, among all the twists and turns of Clinton Administration policy on issues both foreign and domestic, one constant has been an unyielding commitment to abortion-on- demand at home and massive efforts at "population control" abroad. On Clinton's first day in office, which happened to coincide with the twentieth annual "March for Life" in Washington, he signed five executive orders widening the scope of federal involvement with, and funding of, elective abortion. Rigorous pro-Roe litmus tests were applied to all Clinton nominees to the federal judiciary; and few doubted that the Administration wished to see abortion included as a mandated "service" in any national health care reform. Nor, in a time of fiscal restraint, did the Administration hesitate to beef up the population control portion of its foreign assistance budget. Thus ten months after taking office, the President's chief foreign aid administrator, J. Brian Atwood, announced a five-year, $75 million commitment to fund the activities of the International Planned Parenthood Federation. (Mr. Atwood defended these and other population control expenditures on the bizarre grounds that the "core" of the chaos in Somalia, in which U.S. troops were then embroiled, was overpopulation. Somali vital statistics may not be the world's finest, but a reasonable estimate is that Somalia, whose territory is a little larger than that of California, Washington state, Maryland, and Massachusetts combined, had a population in 1992 of some seven million, forty million fewer than the aggregate population of those four states.)

It has never been clear whether the key players in the Clinton Administration really believed that the 42.8 percent of the popular vote they garnered in 1992 constituted a genuine mandate for radical change, or whether that slim plurality impelled the more ideologically fervent members of the Administration to strike while an iron likely to cool quickly was still hot. Whatever the answer, it is indisputably the case that the Administration, led by Undersecretary of State for Global Affairs Timothy Wirth, decided that merely "going beyond Mexico City" was an insufficiently grand goal for the Cairo conference. In league with several Scandinavian and West European countries, UN and World Bank population technocrats, and feminist, anti-natalist, and environmentalist NGOs, the Clintonites sought to engineer a dramatic shift in the focus of the Cairo conference. The packaging ("Population and Development") would remain, but the content would be dramatically altered-with the earth's "carrying capacity," "gender equality, equity, and empowerment of women," and "reproductive rights" supplanting mere "population and development" as the issues of moment. Which amounted, in brief, to a brazen attempt to use international law and the leverage of Western foreign aid programs to establish the sexual revolution, as lived in Stockholm and Hollywood, as the model of humane culture for the twenty-first century.

This radically altered agenda first came into focus in April 1994, when the third meeting of the Cairo conference preparatory committee (Prep-Com III) took place in New York. Among other things, this meeting underscored the ferocity of Undersecretary Wirth and his allies, who were taking no chances that open debate might put sand in the gears of their political machine. The chairman of Prep-Com III, as he would be of the Cairo conference, was Dr. Fred Sai, usually introduced as the "representative of Ghana," but in real life (so to speak), the president of the International Planned Parenthood Federation. Nongovernmental members of the U.S. delegation to the New York session included Bella Abzug, Jeannie Rosoff, president of the Alan Guttmacher Institute (the research arm of Planned Parenthood), Patricia Waak, director of the Audubon Society's population program, and staff members of the Pew Charitable Trusts and the Rockefeller Foundation, two major funders of population control activism. Those who wished to challenge the regnant Clintonite orthodoxies were treated as mere irritants. A seminar sponsored by the United States Catholic Conference, for instance, a registered UN NGO, was denied space in the UN itself; the organizers of the seminar were forbidden to post notice of their meeting; UN officials and population activist NGOs contrived to schedule two other seminars at the same time as the USCC meeting; and meanwhile the shell organization "Catholics for a Free Choice" was given room to operate within the UN complex.

Moreover, this ugliness spilled over from the periphery into the Prep- Com's formal sessions. When Msgr. Diarmuid Martin of the Vatican delegation criticized the proposed Cairo draft document for its ethical hollowness, he was chastised publicly from the chair by Dr. Sai, who complained that the Holy See was trying to foist its notions of sexual morality on the world. Sai's remarks were boisterously applauded by a gallery packed with anti-natalist NGO activists. (Sai's boorish conduct toward the Holy See delegation may have set something of a record for a UN committee chairman, but his anti-Vatican bias was hardly original in substance. At an earlier UN session, Prime Minister Gro Harlem Brundtland of Norway had complained bitterly of obstacles placed in the Cairo conference's path by a "small state with no natural inhabitants.")

It was no surprise, then, that Prep-Com III produced a truly radical draft document for the Cairo conference, in which only six of 118 pages were devoted to the conference's ostensible topic of "population and development," with the bulk of the rest given over to proposals for a lifestyle revolution of awesome proportions.

Not that the classic population controllers did not do well at Prep-Com III. There was no serious challenge to the shibboleths of "overpopulation," and the controllers got a pledge of serious money, the draft document having committed the international community to a massive increase in funding for population control activities, up from the current $6 billion to $17 billion by 2000. (The increase was to be paid for by increased American, Japanese, and Scandinavian contributions to the UN Fund for Population Activities [UNFPA], as well as by cutbacks in UN-sponsored education, health care, industrial development, and disaster relief.)

Still, it was the philosophical shift embedded in the Cairo draft document that marked a sea change in the debate. For the draft document's view of the human condition and the human prospect was rooted in that concept of the radically autonomous individual with which Americans have become all too familiar through the sexual revolution, the deconstructionist decay of the American academy, and the philosophical musings of several Supreme Court justices. "Choice," the mantra of U.S. proponents of abortion-on-demand (along with "gay rights," "alternative forms of marriage," and all the rest of it), became the antiphon of the draft Cairo document produced by Prep-Com III. The results, to put it gently, were striking.

"Marriage" was the dog that didn't bark in the Cairo draft document. In fact, the only time the word "marriage" appeared in the draft document's chapter on "the family" was in a passage deploring "coercion and discrimination in policies and practices related to marriage." But this was hardly surprising, in that the draft document, while frequently noting the importance of "the family in its various forms," said absolutely nothing about the importance of families rooted in stable marriages for the physical and mental well-being of children. Nor did the draft document have much else to say about the natural and moral bond between parents and children and its importance for achieving many of the document's laudable goals, such as improved health care and education for youngsters. Indeed, the document sundered the moral relationship between parents and teenage children by treating sexual activity after puberty as a "right" to be exercised at will, and by suggesting that state population and "reproductive health care" agencies be the primary interlocutors of young men and women coming to grips with their sexuality.

The Cairo draft document also proposed establishing a new category of internationally recognized human rights, viz., "reproductive rights," of which the right to abortion-on-demand was, not surprisingly, the centerpiece. Indeed, it seemed at times as if the codification of an internationally recognized (and, presumably, enforced) "right to abortion" was the primary goal of the Clinton Administration for Cairo. Shortly before Prep-Com III, on March 16, 1994, Secretary of State Warren Christopher had sent a cable to all U.S. diplomatic stations abroad, stating that "the U.S. believes that access to safe, legal, and voluntary abortion is a fundamental right of all women," and emphasizing that the U.S. objective at Cairo was to get "stronger language on the importance" of "abortion services" into the conference final report. Christopher's cable, for all its ignorance of the state of the abortion debate in the U.S., at least had the merit of intelligibility; the draft Cairo document followed the familiar UN pattern of Orwellian euphemism, in which coercive family planning policies became "fertility regulation," and abortion-on-demand was transmuted into "safe motherhood" and "reproductive rights."

In a contradiction familiar to U.S. veterans of the abortion wars, the Cairo draft document then married the philosophy of the imperial autonomous self to a program of large-scale state coercion in the service of "reproductive rights," "gender equity," and, of course, population control. Further, the draft document mandated states to override parental prerogatives (known, in UN-speak, as "social barriers to sexual and reproductive health information and care") in the matter of adolescent sexual education. The draft document also called for state intrusion into the doctor-patient relationship: after warning that "health care providers" must not "restrict the access of adolescents to the services and information they need," the document required states to ensure that those "providers" have the proper "attitudes" toward their teenage patients. One need not doubt that the "attitudes" to be enforced here were those of Dr. Joycelyn Elders. (Undersecretary Wirth seemed particularly exercised on the subject of teenage sexuality. At the conclusion of one session with a senior Vatican official prior to the Cairo conference, Wirth is said to have summed up his case in these pellucid terms: "Young people have to know about their bodies.")

The draft document produced by Prep-Com III also had a nasty totalitarian edge to it. In a striking passage that reflected the affinity between the Kultur of Oprah Winfrey, Phil Donahue, and Linda Bloodworth-Thomasson, on the one hand, and the agenda of Bella Abzug and International Planned Parenthood, on the other, governments were instructed to "use the entertainment media, including radio and television soap operas and drama, folk theater, and other traditional media" to proselytize for the draft document's ideology and "program of action." And in order to insure that the usual male reprobates got the word, the draft document instructed governments to get the message of "reproductive rights" and "gender equity" out by instituting programs that "reach men in their workplaces, at home, and where they gather for recreation," while adolescent boys should be "reached through schools, youth organizations, or wherever they congregate." In sum, there was to be no area of life-home, workplace, gym, ballpark-into which state- sponsored propaganda on "reproductive rights and reproductive health" did not intrude.

Those of us who had thought that this approach to public policy had been consigned to the trash heap of history in 1989 had evidently been mistaken.

III

Given their success at Prep-Com III, the smugness and even arrogance displayed by the UN and Clinton Administration planners of the Cairo conference was, if not exactly admirable, quite understandable. They seemed to have perfected a modus operandi that would enable them to steamroller Cairo in the same way (an expectation that was doubtless further enhanced by the fact that more than sixty representatives of International Planned Parenthood would be coming to Cairo as official delegates from many countries). Not only would Cairo "go beyond Mexico City"; it would adopt the radicals' lifestyle agenda without too much fuss and bother. Critics like the Holy See could easily be brushed aside, as they had been in New York.

Yet even before the Cairo conference convened on Labor Day 1994, some cracks in the coalition that the conference planners were counting on began to show. In the United States-and most especially in the higher altitudes of the Clinton Administration-it is simply assumed that the "empowerment of women," abortion-on-demand, the libertine mores of the sexual revolution, and government propaganda (even coercion) on family planning go hand-in-glove. However, that is not necessarily the way things work in other parts of the world, or even, for that matter, among the truly radical radicals in the West. Thus, in the wake of Prep-Com III, certain feminist organizations, of a far more belligerent kidney than, say, the National Organization for Women, began planning mock trials, to take place in Cairo, of the World Bank, International Planned Parenthood, and the UNFPA, charging them with oppressing women through coercive governmental birth control programs. As it was to turn out, the feminist sans-culotterie could not win; but they were harbingers of an unanticipated irony in the outcome of the conference.

In any case, the most consequential thing that the planners of the Cairo conference had failed to take into account was the moral power of Pope John Paul II. That the Cairo conference did not adopt, but in fact rejected, key aspects of its planners' agenda was the result of a variety of factors: nervousness in Latin America, resistance from Islamic societies, and resentment in certain African countries of what they saw as Western cultural imperialism. But the sine qua non of the defeat suffered by the international advocates of the sexual revolution was the public campaign of opposition to the Cairo draft document mounted throughout the summer of 1994 by John Paul II.

This was not a voluble campaign; in its public (as distinguished from private, i.e., diplomatic) dimension, it consisted of a series of twelve ten-minute reflections that the Pope offered at his public audiences during June, July, and August 1994. But by identifying the fundamental ethical errors of the draft document's approach, and by defining a compelling moral alternative to UN-sponsored libertinism, John Paul II set in motion a resistance movement with considerable potency.

In these reflections, the Pope emphasized that the right to life is the basic human right, "written in human nature," and the foundation of any meaningful scheme of "human rights"; spoke of the family as the "primary cell" of society and as a "natural institution" with rights that any just state must respect; defined marriage "as a stable union of a man and a woman who are committed to the reciprocal gift of self and open to creating new life, [which] is not only a Christian value, but an original value of creation"; defended the equal human dignity of women, insisted that women must not be reduced to being objects of male pleasure, and argued that "perfection for woman is not to be like man, making herself masculine to the point of losing her specific qualities as a woman"; noted that sexuality has a "language of its own at the service of love and cannot be lived at the purely instinctual level"; argued that stable marriages were essential for the welfare of children; pointed out that the Church does not support an "ideology of fertility at all costs," but rather proposes a marital ethic in which the decision "whether or not to have a child" is not "motivated by selfishness or carelessness, but by a prudent, conscious generosity that weighs the possibilities and circumstances, and especially gives priority to the welfare of the unborn child"; rejected coercive or "authoritarian" family planning programs as a violation of the married couple's basic human rights and argued that the foundations of justice in a state are undermined when it does not recognize the unborn child's moral claim to protection; declared that discrimination against women in "workplace, culture, and politics" must be eliminated in the name of an "authentic emancipation" that does not "deprive woman herself of what is primarily or exclusively hers"; and argued that radical individualism is inhuman, as is a "sexuality apart from ethical references."

Throughout the summer of 1994, Undersecretary Wirth continued to insist that "we have no fight with the Vatican." Nonetheless, an argument of considerable amperage had clearly been engaged. In the wake of the confrontation with the Holy See's delegation at Prep-Com III, Wirth himself began a tour of the American hierarchy, focusing on the resident U.S. cardinals. It would not be unrealistic to suggest that in addition to explaining the Administration's position, the Undersecretary was searching for a weak link in the chain of American Catholic episcopal support for John Paul II and the Holy See. He did not find it. Instead, a letter to President Clinton from the then six resident U.S. cardinals (Hickey of Washington, Bernardin of Chicago, Law of Boston, O'Connor of New York, Bevilacqua of Philadelphia, Mahony of Los Angeles), joined as a co-signatory by the president of the National Conference of Catholic Bishops (NCCB), Archbishop William H. Keeler of Baltimore, was hand-delivered to the White House. The letter expressed the prelates' grave concern over "your Administration's promotion of abortion, contraception, sterilization, and the redefinition of the family" and urged the President to reverse the Administration's "destructive" agenda for Cairo. In addition, the NCCB unanimously adopted a statement in which the bishops, as "religious leaders and as U.S. citizens," declared themselves "outraged that our government is leading the effort to foster global acceptance of abortion." And lest it be thought that worries over Cairo were exclusively Catholic, it should be noted that eleven evangelical leaders, including Charles Colson, James Dobson, Charles Swindoll, Billy Melvin, and Bill Bright, cosigned a letter of their own urging the President "not to make the United States an exporter of violence and death."

By the end of the summer, the Pope's decisive clarification of the moral issues at stake in Cairo had not only put the impending conference on the front pages of the prestige press, it had also had a powerful political effect. Undersecretary Wirth, by now a somewhat improbable figure, continued to plead, against all the evidence, that the administration had "no fight with the Vatican." But his superiors evidently disagreed, and were even more evidently worried; for on August 25, Vice President Al Gore, who was to lead the U.S. delegation in the early days of the Cairo conference, gave a speech at the National Press Club in Washington in which he stated that "the U.S. has not sought, does not seek, and will not seek to establish any international right to abortion." Any attempt to suggest otherwise was a "red herring." Yet, as the Holy See's press spokesman, Joaquin Navarro-Valls, pointed out at a press conference in Rome a few days later, Gore's statement did not square with the draft document, whose definition of "reproductive health care" as including "pregnancy termination" had been a U.S. initiative. (Navarro-Valls, in what was perhaps an exercise of charity, did not point out that Gore's Press Club speech was also inconsistent with the Christopher cable of March 16, with the Administration's domestic policy, and with its foreign aid programs.)

There is some reason to believe that the Vice President was misinformed, rather than deliberately disingenuous, on these matters. And no doubt the Vice President was genuinely concerned about charges of administration anti-Catholicism, reignited when a Reuters story of August 19 quoted Faith Mitchell, the State Department's population coordinator, as blaming Vatican disagreement with the Cairo draft document on "the fact that the conference is really calling for a new role for women, calling for girls' education and improving the status of women."* But whatever else it clarified or obscured, the Gore/Navarro-Valls exchange made it unmistakably clear that a great battle loomed in Cairo, where the "private sector advisers" to the U.S. delegation included Pamela Maraldo, president of Planned Parenthood of America and, in what the Administration may inexplicably have thought was a concession to religious concerns, the Rev. Joan Brown Campbell, general secretary of the National Council of Churches.

Perhaps the less ideological and more politically astute members of the U.S. delegation hoped that the moral issues could somehow be finessed. But on the very first day of the conference, any such hopes were dashed: Prime Minister Benazir Bhutto of Pakistan-unmistakably a woman, unmistakably Harvard-educated, and unmistakably a major political figure-took to the rostrum, defended the "sanctity of life" on religious grounds, and condemned the Cairo draft document for trying to "impose adultery, sex education . . . and abortion" on all countries. Predictably, the media gave more attention to distaff Norwegian prime minister Brundtland's defense of "choice" as the essence of the moral issue of abortion. But Bhutto's impassioned rejection of abortion-on- demand, featured on page one of both the *New York Times* and the *Washington Post* and accompanied by pictures of the Pakistani and Norwegian leaders, easily won the battle of feminist iconography-and should have rebutted, once and for all, the charge that the Vatican was holding up consensus on the Cairo document for narrow sectarian reasons.

The opening day statements were followed by five days of negotiating impasse on the document's abortion language, its discussion of the family, and its approach to adolescent sexuality. During that first week, anti-Catholic sentiment and decidedly undiplomatic criticism of the Holy See were freely vented by NGO activists and official delegates alike. Nicolaas Biegman, the Dutch conference vice chairman, complained after four days that "all we read [about] is abortion, abortion, abortion. I deeply regret it. I think it's a pity." Columbia University's Allan Rosenfield, who represented the American College of Obstetricians and Gynecologists, opined that "the Catholic women of the world do not buy into statements from the elderly celibate clergy." Another expert in ecclesiology, Alexander Sanger, president of Planned Parenthood of New York City, told the *New York Times* that "there are two churches, one where the hierarchy talks to the presidents of countries, and then there's the church of the people. The people are picking and choosing what parts of Catholicism they want to carry over to their personal lives." Colombia's Miguel Trias, who heads a government-sponsored family planning organization, fretted that "these Latin American countries are trying to make the Vatican happy. But in 2,000 years the Vatican has never been happy."

Nor was this kind of unpleasantness limited to press conferences. Gail Quinn, a member of the Holy See delegation and executive director of the U.S. bishops' Pro-Life Secretariat, was booed and hissed in a formal session of the conference when she rose to explain the Vatican's objections to some abortion language in the proposed final report; the delegate from Benin had to admonish the chair, the ubiquitous Dr. Sai, that free speech was supposed to be sacrosanct in UN deliberations. Later, while walking past two American representatives in a "delegates- only" area of the conference Center, Quinn heard one of the Americans say to another, in a deliberately audible stage whisper, "There goes that bitch."

All of which should have suggested, at least to the knowledgeable, that the Holy See's delegation was having a considerable impact at Cairo. As, indeed, it was. For contrary to reports in the Times and elsewhere that the Holy See had suffered a significant setback, by the end of the first week of the Cairo conference, the Vatican had in fact achieved a great deal. The final report now stated, unambiguously, that "in no case should abortion be promoted as a method of family planning." The notion of enshrining abortion-on-demand as an internationally recognized basic human right-the centerpiece of the Wirth approach to Cairo-had been abandoned by its proponents, who tacitly conceded that there was no international consensus supporting the claim. The rights and responsibilities of parents in respect of their teenage children had been reaffirmed, and the worst of the euphemistic language about the structure of the family had been changed, so that the Cairo document could not credibly be appealed to on behalf of "gay marriage" and other innovations.

The last major sticking point involved the "safety" of abortions-an important question for the Holy See, which believes that no abortion can be "safe" since, by definition, it results in the death of an innocent human being. The language in dispute stated that "in circumstances where abortion is legal, such abortion should be safe." At the level of moral principle, this was clearly unacceptable to the Vatican, being as it was the equivalent of saying that "in circumstances where female circumcision is legal, it should be performed with novocaine." The language was finally altered to read, "in circumstances where abortion is not against the law, such abortion should be safe"-on the surface a minor change, but one that holds out the prospect of legal reform and that does not concede the rectitude of permissive abortion laws.

The *New York Times* insisted on reporting these debates as a matter of "the Vatican and its few remaining allies" obstructing the course of human progress. But there were other dynamics at work at Cairo, as at

Budapest and Mexico City, and it seemed possible that they could frustrate the more ambitious plans of both population controllers and lifestyle radicals in the future. The controllers' agenda (one of whose historic roots is, frankly, a set of eugenic phobias about "those kind of people") continues to cause serious concern in Latin America, Africa, and Asia, where political leaders understand that it is their populations, not that of, say, Norway, which are to be brought "under control." The resistance of Islamic, Latin American, and some African countries to the libertinism enshrined in the Cairo draft document was also of significance for the future. One need not admire many aspects of life in those societies to applaud their recognition that the sexual revolution's promises of a permissive cornucopia (in Zbigniew Brzezinski's telling phrase) are a snare and a delusion. And, as that recognition becomes increasingly widespread in an America struggling with unprecedented levels of illegitimacy, welfare dependency, and spousal and child abuse, we may also see a dramatic change in our domestic politics. For as the Clinton Administration's defeat at Cairo graphically illustrates, you cannot have it both ways: you cannot strengthen the family and the serious moral commitments necessary to sustain the family by treating the community of father, mother, and children as one option in a limitless menu of "lifestyle alternatives."

Over the long haul, though, the most significant development at the Cairo conference may have been that of a shift in controlling paradigms: from "population control" to "the empowerment of women." As one Indonesian delegate put it toward the end of the meeting, "We have stopped calling women the receptors of contraceptives. We now call them agents of change." Americans long familiar with the alliance between feminism and libertinism may instinctively regard this shift, with reason, as simply an amplification of the moral crisis of modernity. But at Cairo there were interesting suggestions that, in different cultural and historical contexts, the issue of "empowerment" may not cut the way it does in Western Europe and in some parts of the United States.

Benazir Bhutto's speech was one example of that intriguing possibility. For Bhutto's very presence at Cairo, coupled with the content of her remarks, posed a sharp question: why should the "empowerment of women" be necessarily linked to the codification in international law (and national statutes) of the sexual revolution? Who says "A" does not necessarily have to say "B"-at least in non-Western cultures and traditional societies. (Indeed, it is worth remembering that American and Western European pro-life feminists, the vast majority of whom are deeply committed Christians, have resolutely declined to say "B.") Perhaps the question can be pressed even further, though: in the developing world, why shouldn't "the empowerment of women"- meaning that women should be educated, healthy, and no longer treated as property for purposes of marriage- serve to strengthen the roles of women as wives, mothers, and primary educators of their children? Might "the empowerment of women," in cultures whose women would regard Bella Abzug and Pamela Maraldo as something like aliens from Alpha Centauri, lead to a revitalization of the traditional family and a reaffirmation of the distinctively maternal power of women?

Joan Dunlop, president of the International Women's Health Coalition, found it "really extraordinary that in an international UN forum we are talking about sexual and reproductive health and the empowerment of women. These are things that many people of different cultures can understand." Indeed. But the question is, how? The travail of the conference translators at Cairo suggests the volatility of this "empowerment" language (and the rest of the armamentarium of fem-speak) and the difficulty of predicting precisely how it will shape lives in radically different societies and cultures.

French translators had to resuscitate a nineteenth-century term (sante genesique) in the effort to render "reproductive health" in their language. "Family leave" had almost everybody but the Americans stumped; the Arabic translation refers to parents leaving each other after a birth, while the Russian translation spoke of the entire family taking a vacation together. The Chinese thought "sexual exploitation" was an easy one, for they could rely on Chairman Mao's critique of capitalists. (They could also have used his doctor's memoirs, in which the chairman is remembered as an unregenerate sexual predator who ingested ground elks' horns as an antidote to impotence.) But the Arabs were caught between American buzz words and their own religious sensibilities. "Sexually active unmarried individuals"—who are committing criminal acts under Islamic law—thus became "sexually active as-yet-to-be married individuals." The Russians couldn't figure out how to translate "unwanted pregnancies" so that the phrase did not denote "undesirable pregnancies"; and that was relatively mild, compared to the Russian translation of "reproductive health," which comes out as "health that reproduces itself again and again" (the Arabic cuts even closer to the bone of the abortion issue, as "reproductive health" becomes "health concerning the begetting of children").

One veteran population activist, Jason Finkle of the University of Michigan, worried that "all kinds of things have now been packed into the trunk of population: women's and children's health, female literacy, women's labor rights. I'm fearful that we've gotten away from the focus on population size and growth." It does not seem, after Cairo, an entirely unreasonable expectation. But some will regard this as something less to be feared than to be-very cautiously-celebrated.

IV

Some things that ought to have happened at Cairo didn't. There was no concerted challenge to the ideologically charged concept of "overpopulation," although the work of Nicholas Eberstadt, Julian Simon, Karl Zinsmeister, and others has made clear that the term itself has no credible scientific meaning. This intellectual failure, combined with the clash of moral visions at Cairo, produced a somewhat schizoid final document, which endorses voluntary measures of population control but then sets population targets whose achievement would seem to require coercive governmental intervention in family planning. The resolution of that tension will, over the next decade, tell us much about the future of population policy (and politics) at both the international and national levels.

The conference also failed to confront the UN's continuing fixation on Third World development as essentially a matter of massive resource transfers from the developed to the developing world. The Holy See did heroic work at Cairo, and in the months between Prep-Com III and the September conference. But it would have added even more to the debate had its representatives taken up the question of governmental criminality and its relationship to the despoilation of the Third World; materials for such a challenge were ready to hand in the 1987 encyclical of John Paul II, Solicitudo Rei Socialis, in which the Pope had urged developing nations to "reform certain unjust structures, and in particular their political institutions, in order to replace corrupt, dictatorial, and authoritarian governments with democratic and participatory ones." The Holy See might also have taken a leaf from John Paul's 1991 social encyclical Centesimus Annus and boldly urged the view that human beings are the basic resource for development, because the source of wealth in the modern world is human creativity.

At the grassroots level, it will be a while before the paradigm shift from "population control" to "empowerment of women" takes effect. Meanwhile, huge amounts of money will continue to be poured into family planning programs, many of which are either subtly or overtly coercive. Remedial action on this front will require extreme vigilance over foreign aid budgets, and careful attention will have to be paid to the Clinton Administration as it tries to square its adherence to an international agreement that flatly rejects abortion as a means of family planning with its commitment to huge increases in U.S. aid funding to organizations that actively promote precisely that evil.

So the Battle of Cairo will continue, in other venues. And it will remain, at bottom, a moral struggle: about the dignity and value of human beings, about the rights and responsibilities of women and men, about the relationship between marriage, sexuality, and the rearing of children. Thanks to John Paul II's refusal to concede the Holy See's irrelevance in accordance with the prepared media script, the unavoidable moral core of the population argument was forced onto center stage at Cairo. And there it became clear, to those with eyes to see, that the mores of Hollywood, Manhattan's Upper West Side, and Copenhagen are not universally shared, admired, or sought.

That, in itself, was no mean accomplishment. And it might, just might, presage a more morally and empirically serious population and development debate in the future.

In the same Reuters report in which Ms. Mitchell suggested that the Church wanted to deny women an education, State Department spokesman Mike McCurry warned the Vatican against negotiating with Iran. A week later, in Cairo, American delegates were seen openly negotiating compromise language on abortion and "reproductive rights" with Iranian delegates.

George Weigel, a member of the editorial board of *First Things*, is president of the Ethics and Public Policy Center in Washington, D.C.

The Development of Feminism from the Renaissance Period to the Modern Age

Based on the work of Sr. Prudence Allen, RSM, PhD

I. Renaissance Feminism
    A.   Representative Authors:
        1.   Christine de Pizan (1363-1431)
        2.   Francesco Barbaro (1390-1454)
        3.   Albrecht von Eyb (1420-1466)
        4.   Henricus Cornelius Agrippa (1486-1535)
        5.   Lucrezia Marinella (1571-1653)
        6.   Juan Luis Vives (1492-1540)
        7.   Marie le Jars de Gournay (1565-1645)
    B.   Characteristics of Renaissance feminism:
        1.   Identified as obstacles for women's full development:
            a.   Satirical attitudes of men towards women and marriage
            b.   Lack of access for women to higher education
        2.   Early Renaissance feminists defended women's capacity for fidelity
        3.   All but one chose sacramental marriage or clerical state
        4.   Promoted complementarity, reverse polarity and traditional polarity theories of gender identity [see Sr. Prudence Allen's, RSM, PhD's chart at end of outline]

II. Enlightenment Feminism
    A.   Representative Authors:
        1.   René Descartes as founder (1596-1650)
        2.   Anna Maria van Schurman (1607-1678) and Reformation in the Netherlands
        3.   François Poullain de La Barre (1647-1723) and Reformation in Geneva
        4.   Mary Astell (1666-1731), John Locke and Reformation in England
        5.   Mary Wollstonecraft (1759-1797) and Jean-Jacques Rousseau and Reformation in France and other European locations
        6.   Theodor Gottlieb von Hippel (1741-1796), Immanuel Kant and German Reformation
        7.   Anti-feminists Kierkegaard, Nietzsche, and Hegel and fractional complementarity
    B.   Characteristics of Enlightenment feminism:
        1.   Identified as obstacles for women's full development:
            a.   Lack of equality of women and men
            b.   Lack of access for women to higher education
            c.   The institution of marriage itself as conflicting with higher education and reducing women to property of husband
            d.   Lack of women's right to suffrage and political responsibility
            e.   Limitation of women to intuition and non-rational intelligence
        2.   Defended women's capacity for higher education and political involvement
        3.   Most did not marry, one left priesthood to marry, another married twice
        4.   Attacked Priesthood and Mass and the Catholic Church
        5.   Promoted unisex theory and fractional complementarity (in marriage men and women are like $2/3+1/3$, $3/4+1/4$, $1/2+1/2 = 1$ human being)

III. Post-Enlightenment Feminism
    A.   Marxist Feminism
        1.   Representative Authors:
            a.   Karl Marx (1818-1883) and Frederick Engels (1820-1895)
            b.   Emma Goldman (1869-1940)
            c.   Evelyn Reed
            d.   Marlene Dixon
            e.   Maria dalla Costa and Selma James
            f.   Shulamith Firestone
        2.   Characteristics of Marxist feminism
            a.   Identified as obstacles for women's full development:
               i.   Private property and the Catholic Church
               ii.   Wife as unpaid laborer/property of husband
               iii.   The family

iv.   Pregnancy, reproduction and childbearing
    b.   Defended women's work in the family and outside
    c.   Generally promoted a unisex theory
    d.   Promoted abortion, artificial insemination and means that render women infertile

B.   Existential to Radical Feminism
    1. Representative Authors:
        a.   Simone de Beauvoir (1908-1985)
        b.   Mary Daly
        c.   Monique Wittag, Hélène Cixous, and Julia Kristeva
    2. Characteristics of radical feminism:
        a.   Identified as obstacles for women's full development:
            i.   Men (the other)
            ii.   The Catholic religion and metaphysics
            iii.   Language and gender differentiation
            iv.   The Family
            v.   Pregnancy, reproduction and childbearing
        b.   Promoted reverse gender polarity and/or unisex theories

C.   Secular Feminism
    1. Representative Authors:
        a.   John Stuart Mill (1806-1873) and Harriet Taylor
        b.   Elizabeth Cady Stanton (1815-1902) and Susan B. Anthony (1820-1906)
        c.   Margaret Sanger (1879-1966)
        d.   Ferdinand Schiller (1864-1937) and William James (1842-1910)
        e.   Betty Friedan (1921-2006), The Humanist Manifesto, and NOW
    2. Characteristics of secular feminism:
        a.   Identifies as obstacles for women's full development:
            i.   Unjust marriage laws
            ii.   Unjust laws prohibiting women from suffrage and political life
            iii.   Lack of access to artificial means of rendering women infertile
            iv.   Discrimination prohibiting women's higher education
            v.   Discrimination prohibiting women's access and equal pay for equal work
            vi.   Being a house wife (married to a house)
            vii.   Lack of abortion on demand
        b.   Defends women's full participation in higher education and public life
        c.   Promotes a unisex theory
        d.   Works actively to promote laws that undermine Catholic marriage, the Catholic Church and organized religion

IV. The Catholic Response: Personalist Feminism to New Feminism

A. Representative Authors:
    1. Pope Leo XIII Encyclical *Arcanum. On Christian Marriage* (1880)
    2. Dietrich von Hildebrand (1889-1977)
    3. Pope Pius XI Encyclical *Casti Connubii: On Christian Marriage* (1930)
    4. Bernard Lonergan (1904-1984) "Finality, Love and Marriage"
    5. Edith Stein (1891-1942)
    6. Jacques Maritain (1892-1973) and Raissa Maritain (1893-1960)
    7. Emmanual Mounier (1905-1950)
    8. Pope Pius XII addresses on marriage (1939-1958)
    9. Gabriel Marcel (1889-1973)
    10. Karol Wojtyła/Pope John Paul II (1960-2005)

B. Characteristics of personalist feminism:
    1. Identifies as obstacles for women's full development:
        a.   Lack of adequate metaphysical and anthropological foundations for Catholic marriage
        b.   All forms of discrimination, violence or exploitation against women in the home and in the world
        c.   Naturalistic, hedonistic, and materialistic views of marriage
        d.   Lack of recognition of women's full equal dignity with man
        e.   Lack of respect for woman's and man's significantly unique identities
        f.   Abortion and artificial means that render women infertile
    2. Generally promotes an integral complementarity (in marriage men and women are synergenetically 1 + 1 > > 3
    3. Defends women as especially good in welcoming and fostering the growth of other persons—as humanizing a society where utilitarianism and hedonism are prevalent
    4. Calls on women to build a new feminism that pays attention to the person

STRUCTURE OF THEORIES OF GENDER IDENTITY

Theory	Equal Dignity of Man and Woman	Significant Differentiation of Man and Woman
1. Gender Unity (unisex and unigender)	Yes	No
2a. Traditional Gender Polarity	No Man *per se* superior to woman	Yes
2b. Reverse Gender Polarity	No Woman *per se* superior to man	Yes
3a. Fractional Gender Complementarity	Yes	Yes Complementary as parts
3b. Integral Gender Complementarity	Yes	Yes Complementary as wholes
4. Gender Neutrality	Neutral	Neutral

About the Author

Erica Laethem is currently pursuing a licentiate degree in bioethics at the Pontifical University Regina Apostolorum in Rome. She earned her undergraduate degree in political science at the University of Michigan, where her encounter with the writings of early Protestant reformers and the discovery of the teachings of John Paul II led her back to the Catholic faith.

In March of 2005, Erica provided consultation to national delegations on issues pertaining to human rights and the dignity of woman at the United Nation's "Beijing + 10" Conference on the Status of Women in March of 2005. She serves as the vice-president of The MARVEL Group—the Movement for the Advancement of Rights, Virtue, Education, and Leadership.

Endow *Letter to Women* Study Evaluation

Note: Please fill out this evaluation as *honestly* as possible.

1. What were you hoping to get out of this small study? Did this study fulfill your expectations?Did you learn what you had hoped? What else would you like to know?

2. Did you find the format of the study understandable and easy to follow? If not, what would have made it clearer?

3. What did you like most about this study? What did you like the least? How can ENDOW improve the study?

4. Did you feel comfortable in this small group? If not, what would have made you feel more comfortable?

5. Are you interested in participating in other ENDOW studies? Do you intend to continue with your current group?

6. Please give us any additional comments that you have.

Thank you so very much!